AF609488

MUSEUM OF DOGS

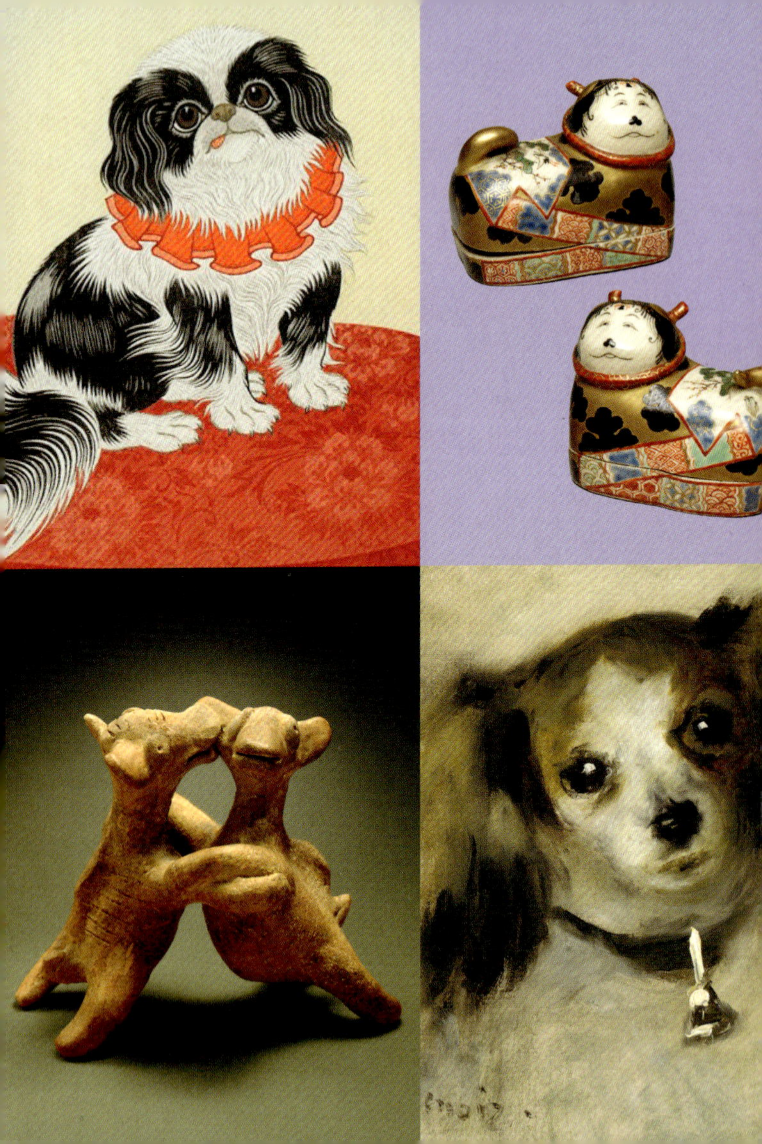

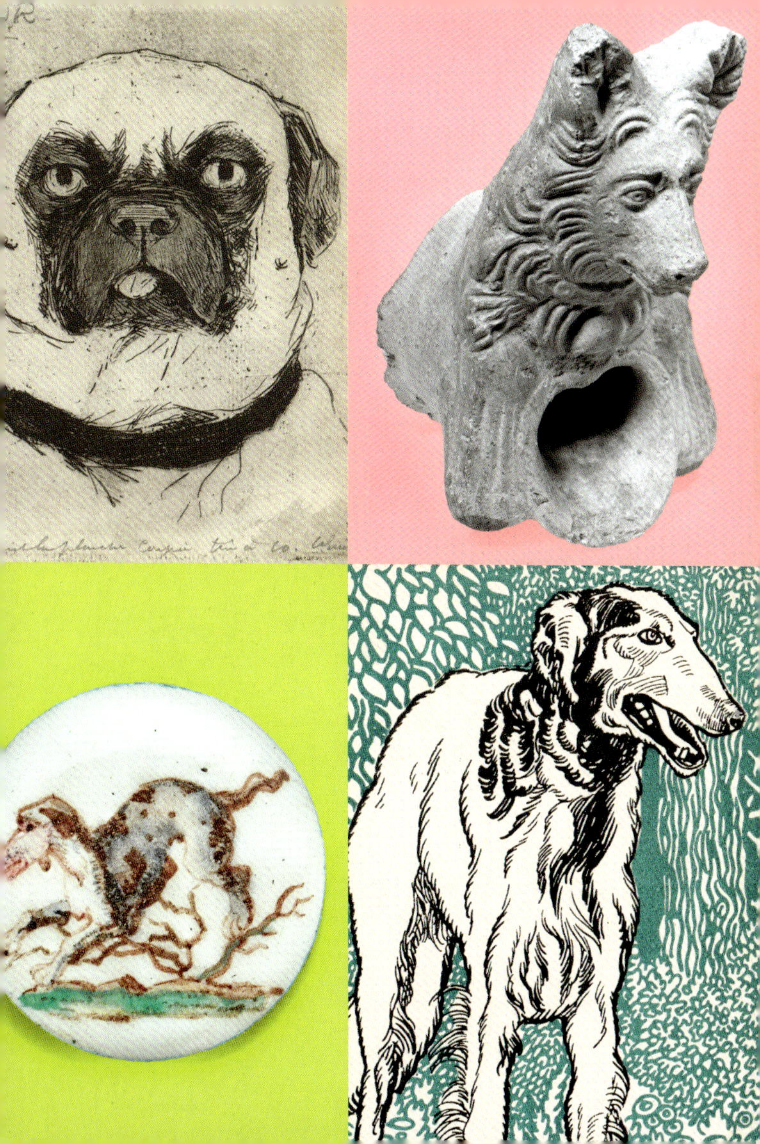

MUSEUM OF DOGS

A ROMP THROUGH ART HISTORY *for* DOG PEOPLE

JESSICA POUNDSTONE

CHRONICLE BOOKS
SAN FRANCISCO

Page 216 constitutes a continuation of the copyright page.

Library of Congress Cataloging-in-Publication Data
Names: Poundstone, Jessica, author.
Title: Museum of dogs : a romp through art history for dog people / Jessica Poundstone. Description: San Francisco : Chronicle Books, [2025] | Includes bibliographical references.
Identifiers: LCCN 2024038154 | ISBN 9781797234243 (hardcover) Subjects: LCSH: Dogs in art.
Classification: LCC N7668.D6 P68 2025 | DDC 704.9/432977—dc23/eng/20240918
LC record available at https://lccn.loc.gov/2024038154

Manufactured in China.

Design by Allison Weiner.
Typesetting by Frank Brayton. Typeset in MFT Milano.

Cover: Émile Gallé, *Figure of a Dog*, 1870–1880, Glazed earthenware, H × W × D: 30.7 × 17 × 26.1 cm ($12\frac{1}{16}$ × $6\frac{11}{16}$ × $9\frac{7}{8}$ in.), Cooper Hewitt, Gift of Anonymous Donor, Smithsonian Design Museum, New York. https://www.si.edu/object/figure-dog:chndm_1967-48-108

10 9 8 7 6 5 4 3 2 1

Chronicle Books LLC
680 Second Street
San Francisco, California 94107
www.chroniclebooks.com

Thank you to my family, Ben, Sophie, and Henry, for enduring and supporting my extreme enthusiasm for this book. And of course to my pug/chihuahua/poodle, Stanley, who was with me literally every moment I was working on this because a) we are super-bonded, b) I work from home, and c) we both love snacks.

I also want to thank the many museums that are not only digitizing their collections, but also making their images available to share for projects like this one.

This book is dedicated to all the wonderful dogs in my life, in particular (in alphabetical order): Artie, Bama, Barney, Bizzy, Bobbin, Buddy, Cheddar, Clem Fandango, Cocoa, Cookie, Coquille, Cuervo, Desmond, Dill, Doug, Elvis, Frida, Grey, Gwillym, Hazelnut, Henry, Higgins, Izzy, Jagger, Kali, Kevin Arnold, Lemon, Locke, Lola, Louise, Lucy, Luna, Marlow, Milkshake, Monkey, Mr. Chubbs, Noodles, Ollie, Penny, Piper, Poppy, Rev, Riggs, Sasha, Shep, Skipper, Stanley, Stella, Taffie, Tiber, Violet, Walter, Wendell, and Zeus, as well as all of the other friends I have (unforgivably) missed.

Love y'all—and your people too.

Hello and welcome, fellow dog person!

Humans have loved dogs since we started hanging out together about fifteen thousand years ago. Curious about what I might find as evidence of our BFF status, I virtually visited dozens of museums around the world. Y'all, I hit the jackpot. On their websites I found many treasures, including paintings, sculptures, jewelry, and so much more. Many of these pieces aren't on display at the museums they live in; they're tucked away in a back room somewhere. That means very few of us would ever get the chance to see them—until now!

In this book I've gathered the dog art and artifacts that charmed, astounded, and delighted me the most. I truly hope they do the same for you.

So go ahead—turn the page! I am so excited for you to meet these dog friends—and learn some quirky facts you can share in virtually any social setting. Prepare to see some dogs so adorable, and from so long ago, you might not be able to believe they exist!

And give your dog (or any nearby dog) a little head scratch for me, won't you?

STATUETTE OF A HOUND GNAWING A BONE

Greek, 3rd–2nd century BC, bronze

It's the second century BC in Greece: Eratosthenes accurately calculates the Earth's circumference. Ctesibius designs the hydraulis, an early version of a pipe organ. And this statuette is made. But doesn't it feel like it could have been made last week? Just a blissed-out dog gnawing on a bone. Timeless.

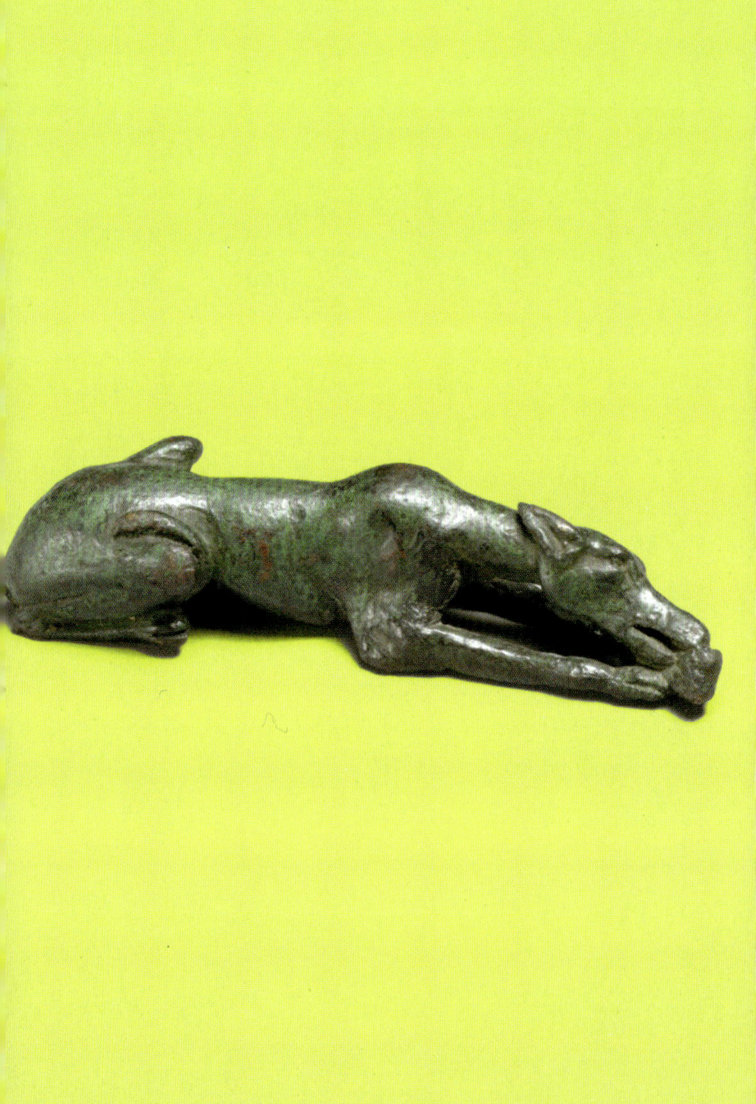

THREE YOUNG DOGS

Attributed to Nakamura Hôchû, Japanese, 1826, color woodcut

If all the little Pokémon characters looked like these three, I would be so into it. Alas.

These portly puppies are part of a book published in 1826, most likely by an artist named Nakamura Hôchû. It contains twenty-six prints in which Nakamura revived a method of painting called *mokkotsu*, which means "boneless." Yaaaaas.[1]

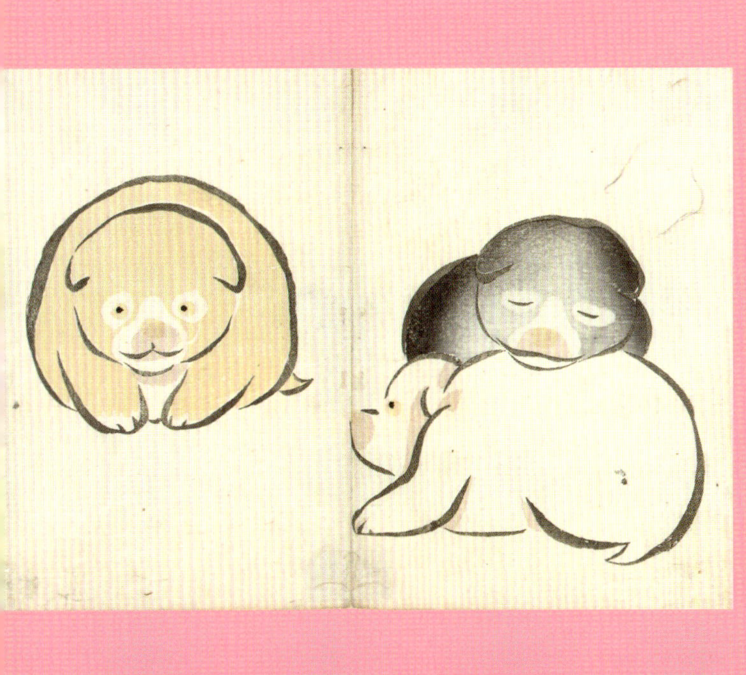

SKETCH OF A DOG

Egyptian, 1295–1070 BC, limestone

Egyptians used chips of limestone with animal images like this one as illustrations when they told stories and jokes. This pup was definitely up to something extremely suspicious and/or goofy in this story.

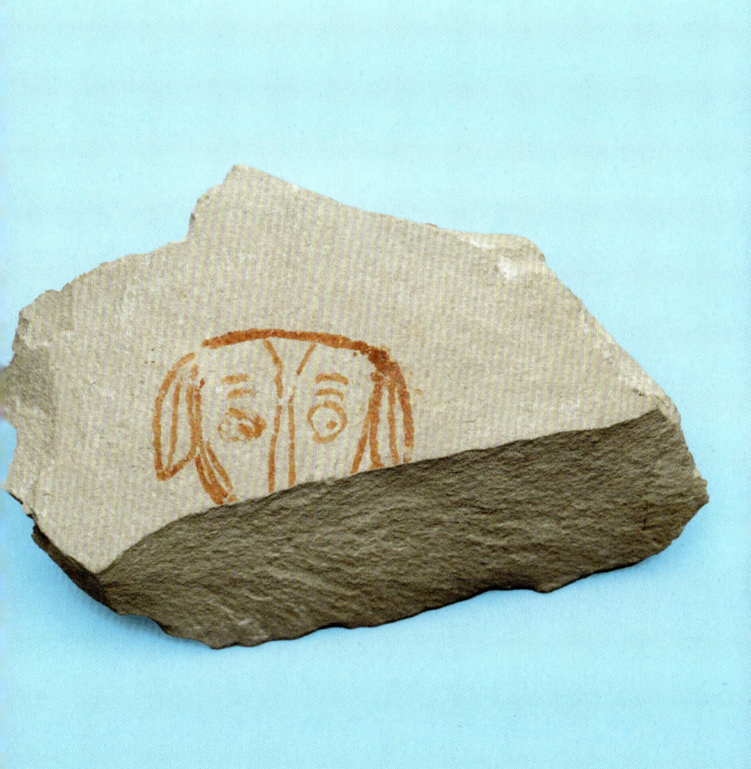

BOX

British, 19th century, enamel on copper

If you had been alive in eighteenth-century England, you might have been gifted a small box like this one with candy in it.

What kind of candy, you ask?

Well, with sugar production up (which drove sugar prices down—see, I was paying attention in econ), Victorian-era folks went a little bonkers inventing new confections, including pear drops, sherbet lemons, cough candy, aniseed twists, marshmallows, candy floss, and fruit gums.

One of each, please (okay, maybe I can do without the cough candy): Put them all in a derpy-dog bonbon box and I will love you forever.[2]

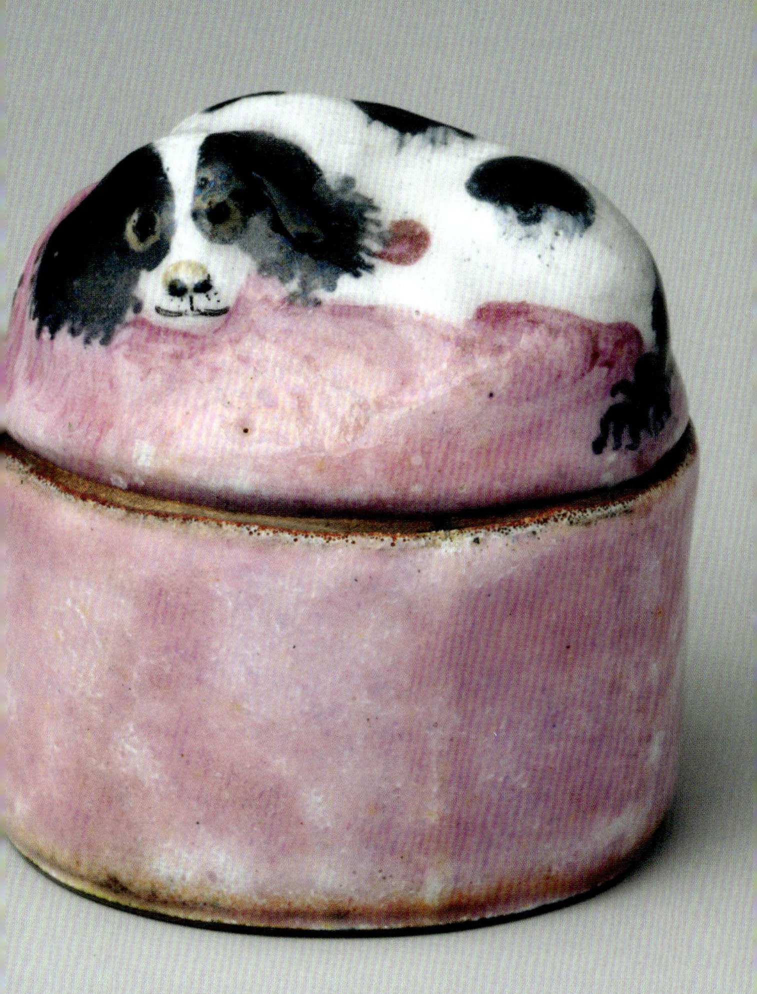

DOG PENDANT

European, 1575–1600, gold, rubies, pearls, and enamel

This pendant was one of many made in the late 1500s where the jeweler used the irregular shape of a pearl as the inspiration for the body of the work.

I'm not sure who would have wanted to wear this pendant, but I am quite sure that I would like to have met them.

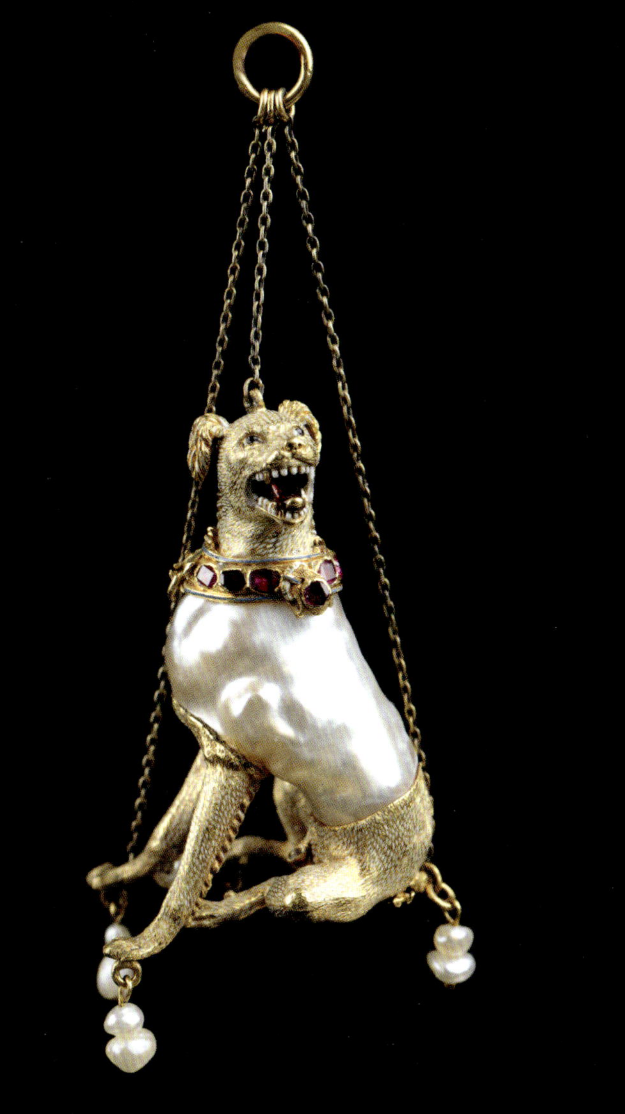

DOG SLED WITH THREE DOGS

Inuit, 19th century, walrus ivory, pigment, string, and animal hide

Inuit carvers believed that amulets had the power to lead hunters to the animals they needed for survival. The detail here is stunning, down to the leather harnesses on the three sled dogs.

Although women weren't typically included in hunting parties, there is a female figure in this work—exciting to see!

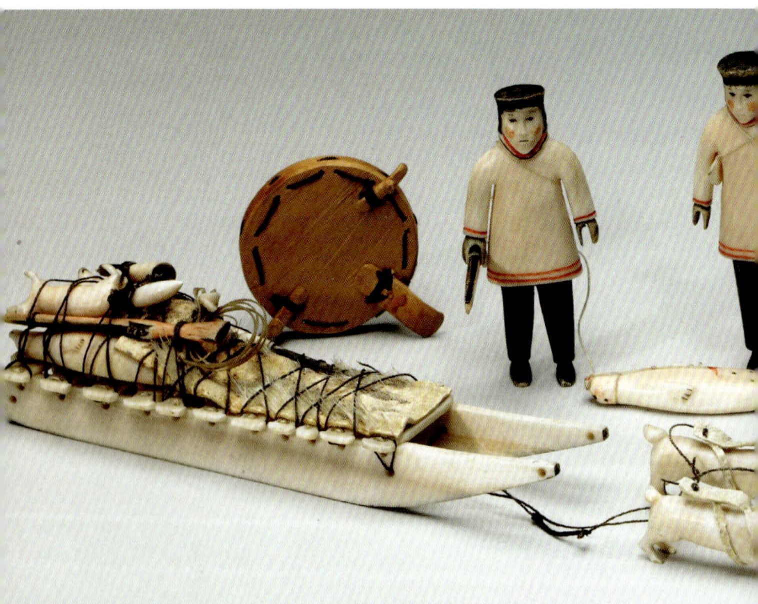

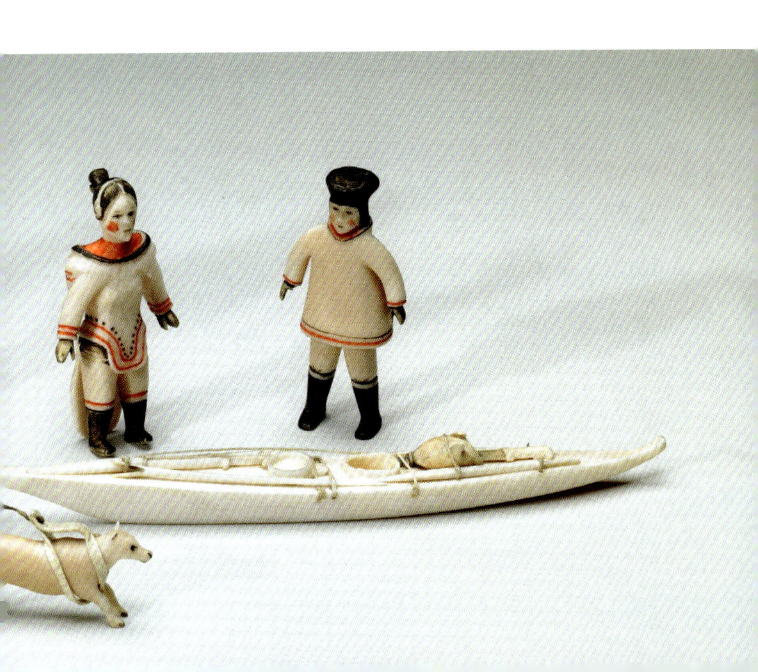

SLEEPING DOG

Bertha van Hasselt, Dutch, 1930, lithograph on paper

Did you know—because I sure did not—that from 1912 to 1948 the Olympics included art competitions in five categories: architecture, literature, music, painting, and sculpture? For works with sports-related themes? Like what?! Bring it back!

Dutch painter and printmaker Bernardina Johanna Roberta (a.k.a. Bertha) van Hasselt entered her work at the 1928 Summer Olympics in Amsterdam. Sadly, she did not medal, but I would definitely have given her the gold for this absolutely delightful Great Dane.[3]

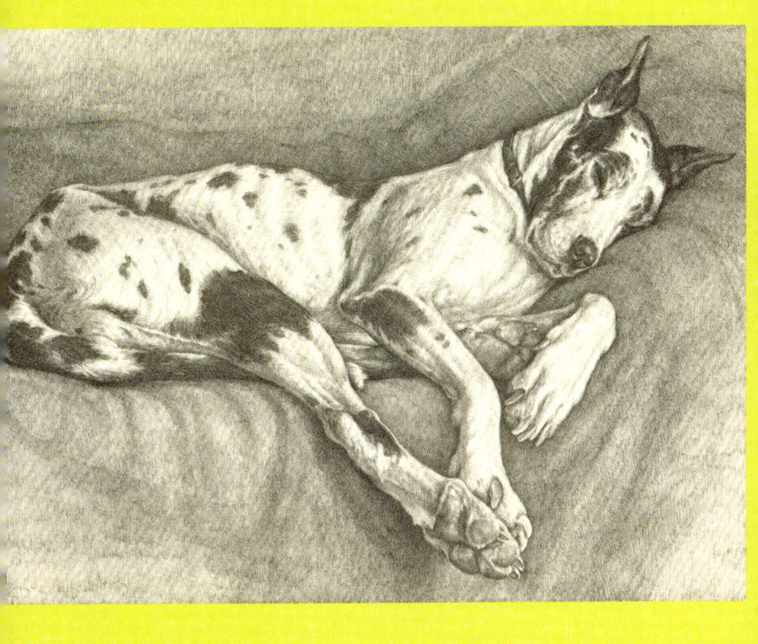

POODLE POWDER BOX

French, 1940, ink and gouache on tracing paper

In 1940, the extremely posh jewelry purveyors Maison Boucheron hired the design firm of Strauss, Allard, and Meyer to come up with ideas for makeup compacts. Tragically, this design does not appear to have been manufactured. But the cases that were made—from pure gold and often featuring precious jewels and intricate, lacy cutouts on the lid—are worth looking up.

Maison Boucheron is still in operation today. Perhaps if we all write to them and ask very nicely they might produce this design for us? It's worth a try.

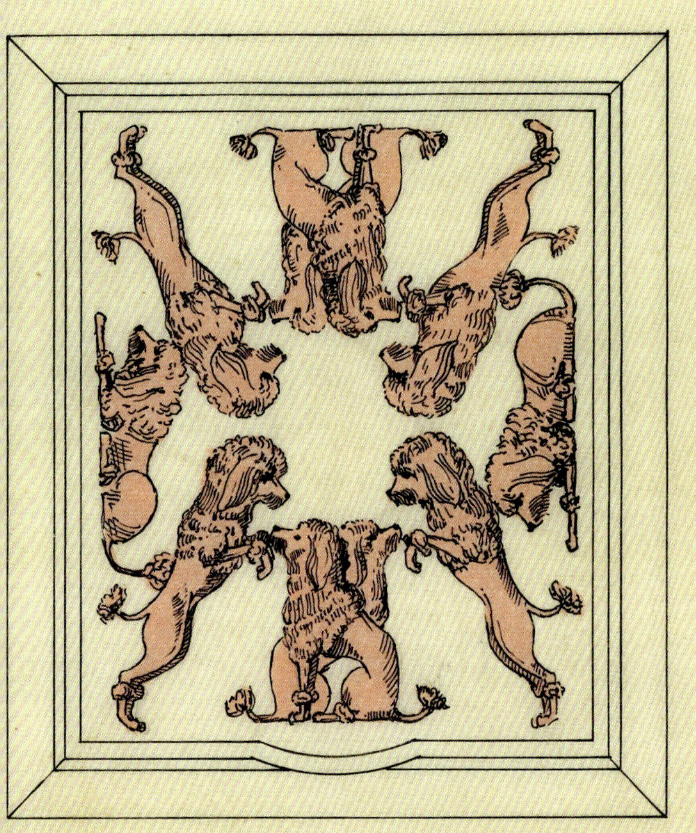

BOLOGNESE TERRIER

Russian, 1811–1850, porcelain

Porcelain was a big deal in Russia during the 1800s, due in part to its promotion by the leaders of the splendidly named Imperial Society for the Encouragement of the Arts in St. Petersburg.

Any organization that encourages the creation of something as majestic as this Bolognese terrier has to be doing something at least a little bit right.

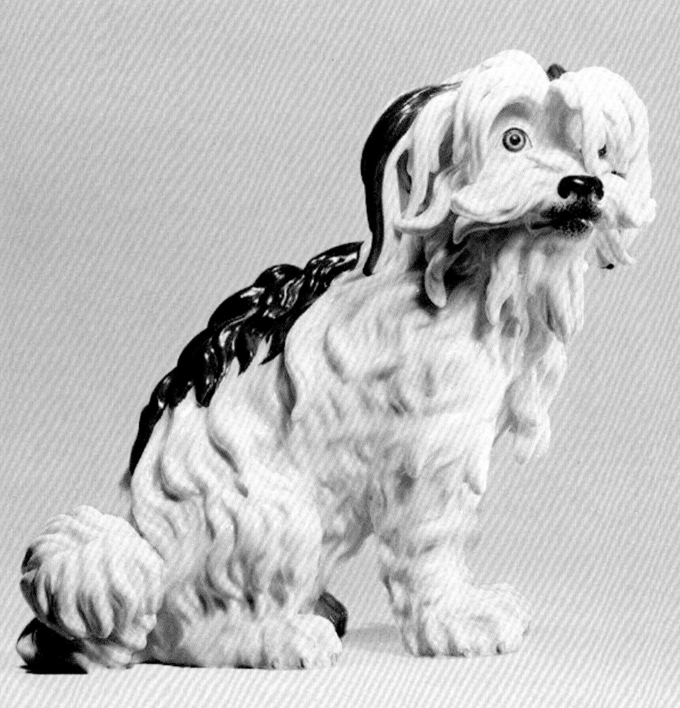

SINGLE SPOUT AND BRIDGE VESSEL IN THE FORM OF A DOG GNAWING A BONE

South American, AD 700–1000, ceramic and pigment

Similar vessels made around 1000 BC—and likely this one as well—were referred to as whistling jars because when you fill them with liquid and tilt them forward, air is forced out, making a sound. So basically, it's a three-in-one portable music device, water bottle, and friend. Take that, smartphones.

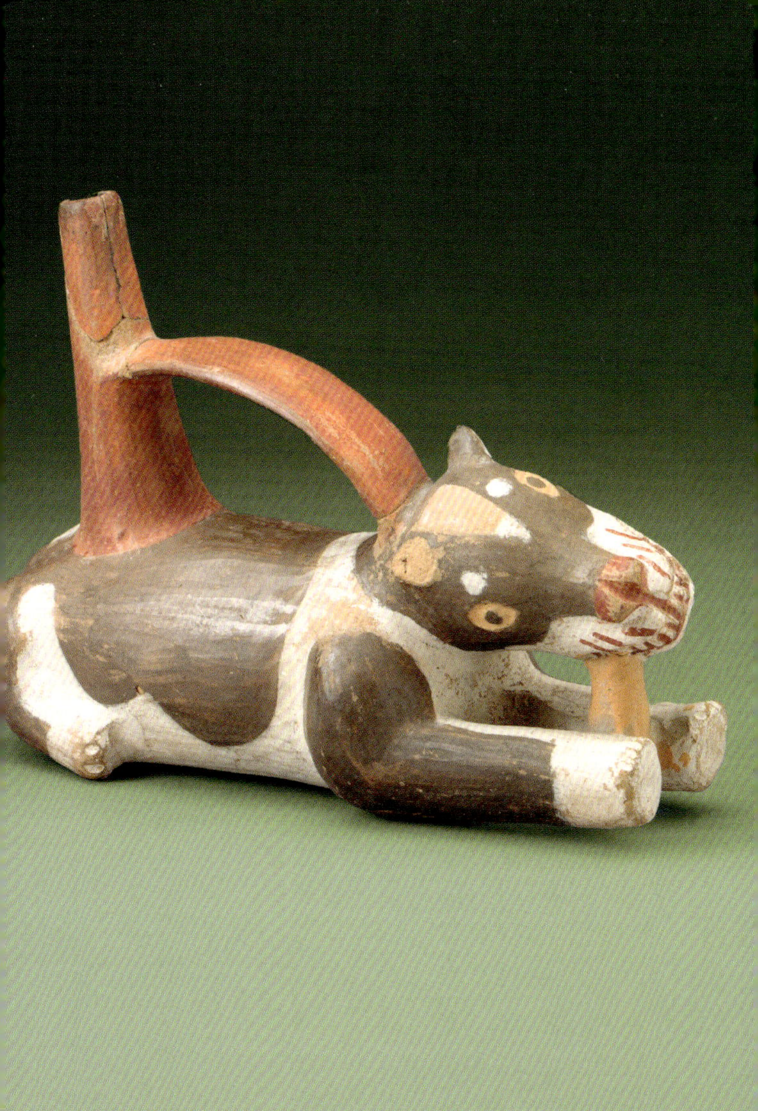

SPECTACLE CASE

Mexican, late 19th century, glass beads, linen, leather, and metal

Someone entrusted this dog with a very important key, so of course you could trust it with your spectacles.

This piece was part of a wide array of beadwork collected by Elizabeth Morrow, Charles Lindbergh's mother-in-law. Elizabeth was married to the United States' ambassador to Mexico, and she was excited to share the loveliness of the art and crafts she found there with the rest of the world.

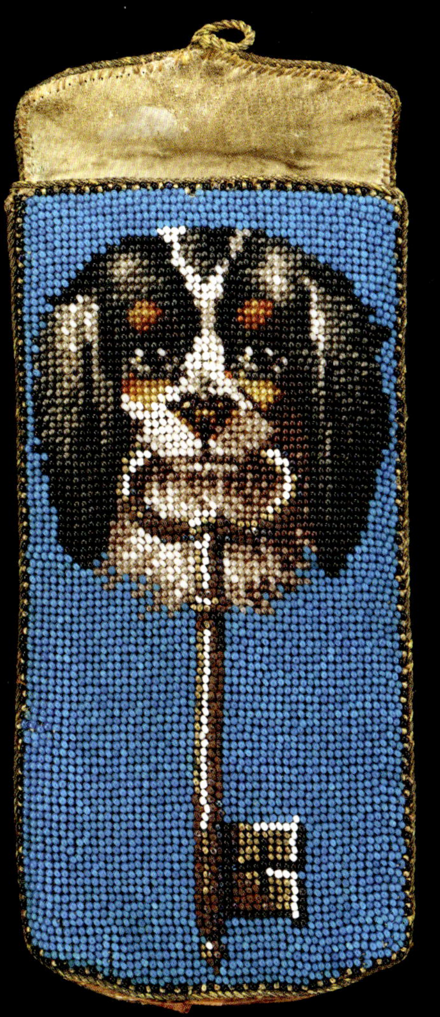

NETSUKE OF DOG ON A STAND

(side and back views)

Japanese, 19th century, red lacquer

Originally, kimonos had no pockets. Women would tuck personal items they wanted to have close at hand—fans, coin purses, mirrors—into their sleeves. Apparently, men were not into that system, but they still needed to be able to carry their stuff—pipes, pens, tobacco pouches—around.

Hence the creation of the *sagemono*, a small satchel on a cord. Essentially, a purse. The cord was wrapped around the kimono's sash and attached using a bead (*ojime*) and a toggle (*netsuke*).

These netsukes got absolutely wild—so intricate! So exquisite! So whimsical! Look them up and you'll see.

I've only got two more words to share about this adorable example: That tail!

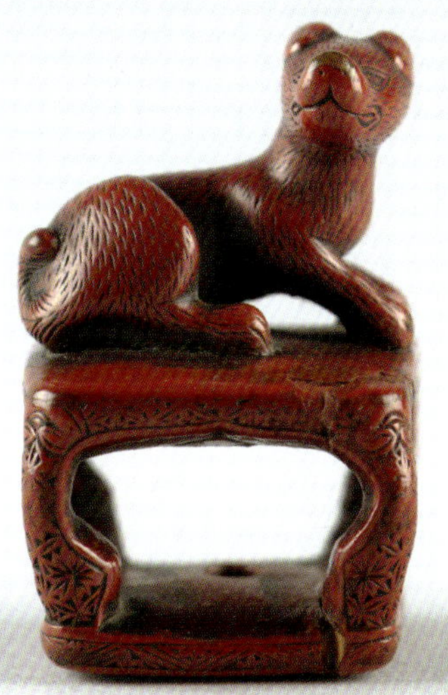

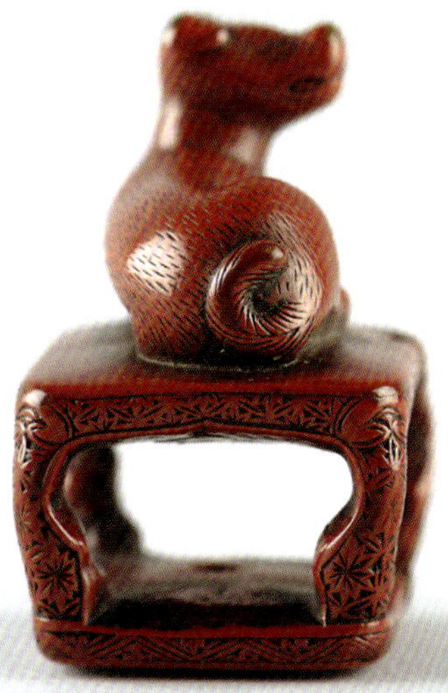

SIBERIAN DOGS IN THE SNOW

Franz Marc, German, 1909, oil on canvas

In a letter to a friend, artist Franz Marc said that he wanted his work to "intensify the aesthetic emotions . . . by blending the painted canvas with the souls of the spectator and the animal." Pretty lofty goal.

In this painting, both the colors and the textures—like a delightful white frosting—emphasize the dogs' oneness with nature. Does your soul feel blended?

Marc's white Siberian sheepdog mix, Russi, was a model for much of his work—including this piece, most likely. Gratuitous additional note: Marc also kept two deer as pets, and their names were Schlick and Hanni.[4]

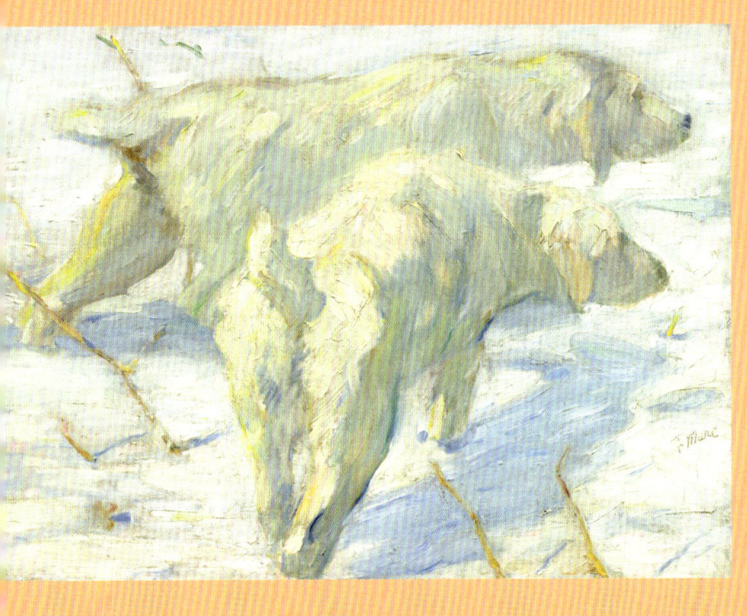
F. Marc

DOG

Japanese, late 17th century, ceramic

A Japanese potter named Sakaida Kakiemon invented the techniques for decorating porcelain with enamel glazes, including the glazes we see in this piece: white, red, blue, and turquoise.

Kakiemon's techniques were lost for a few hundred years but were rediscovered and subsequently declared an Important Intangible Cultural Asset by the Japanese government in 1971. Good save!

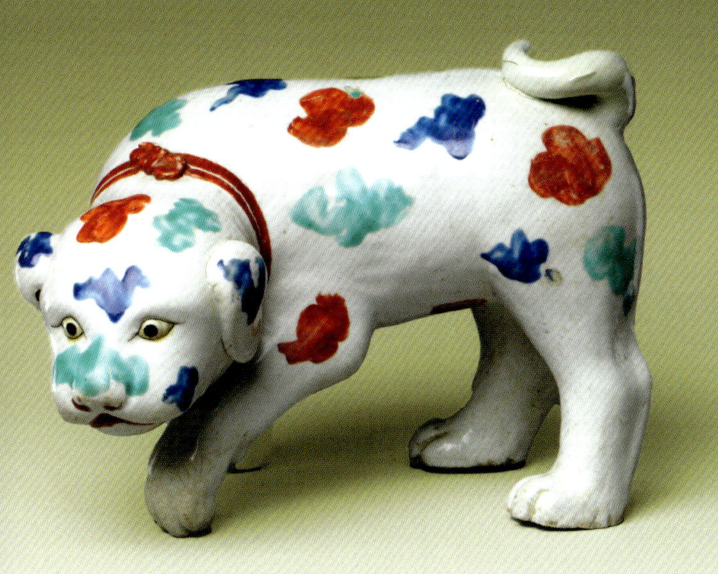

DALMATIAN

American, 20th century, carved wood

This sculpture is so big and sturdy it may have been made for kids to ride on! Come to think of it, I hope this wasn't a substitute for getting them a real dog . . .

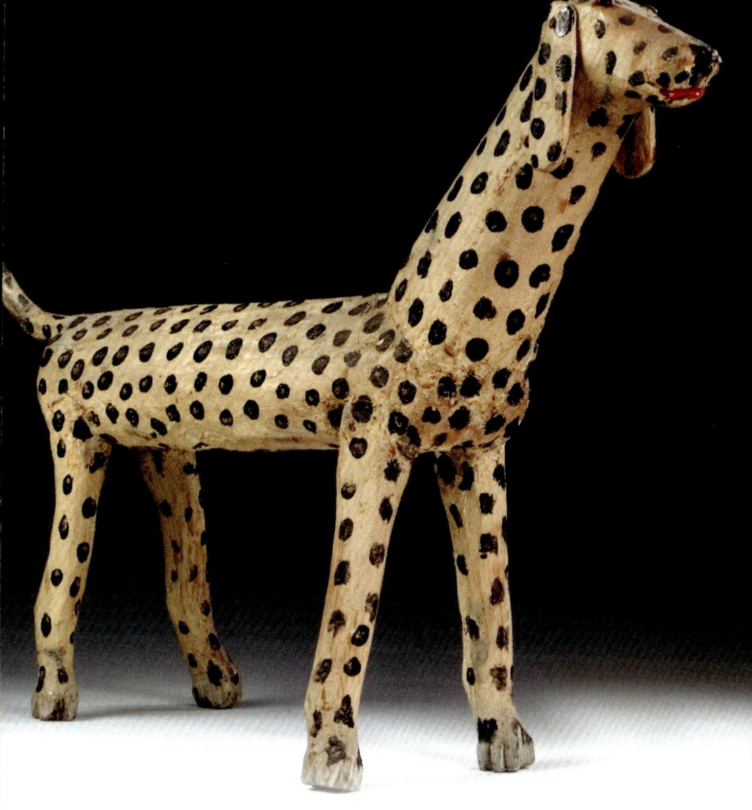

LID

Etruscan, 5th century BC, bronze

This lid may have been made for a deep bowl called a *lebes*, which could be put over a fire for cooking. And a common staple in ancient Greek cuisine was lentils. So perhaps we could, very fancifully, call this a Lab Looking Loyal atop a Lentil Lebes Lid.

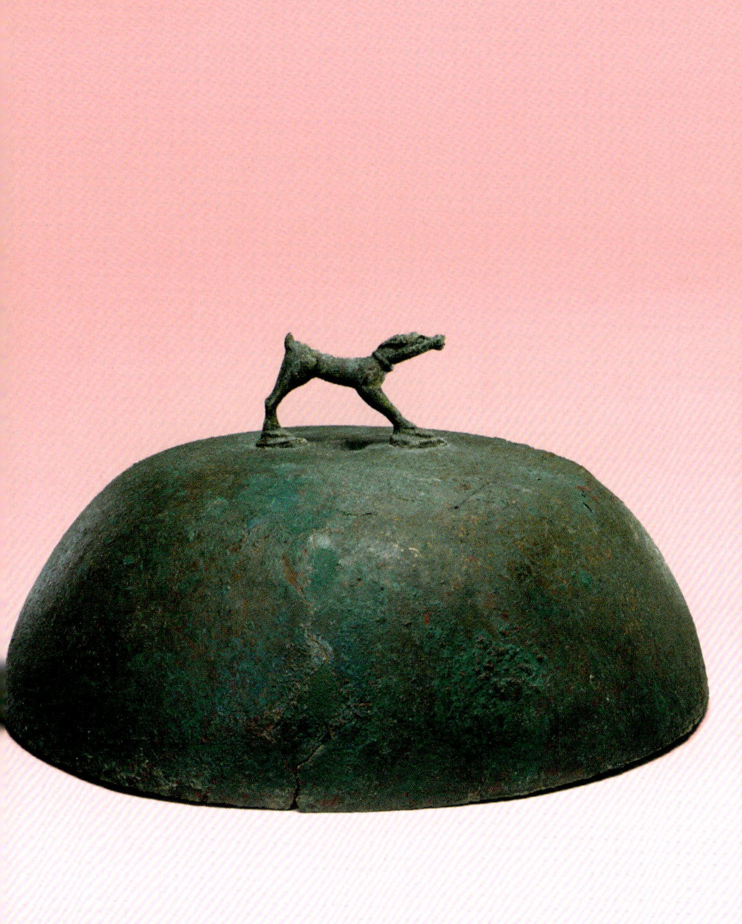

DOG (MANTEL ORNAMENT)

Z. S. Lupus, American, 1938, watercolor

There's evidence in texts and frescoes that in ancient Egypt and Greece spotted dogs ran alongside horse-drawn chariots, so their reputation as endurance runners and horse whisperers started way back.

Centuries later, Dalmatians continued to play to their strengths by working alongside horse-drawn wagons—including the ones firefighters used to get water pumps to a blaze. As an added bonus, Dalmatians also served as sirens, running ahead of the firefighters' wagons and barking to clear the way.

The Dalmatian in this watercolor, probably intended for production as a statuette, looks more like an indoorsy kinda guy, but I'm pretty sure his intense side-eye could clear a room if the need arose.[5]

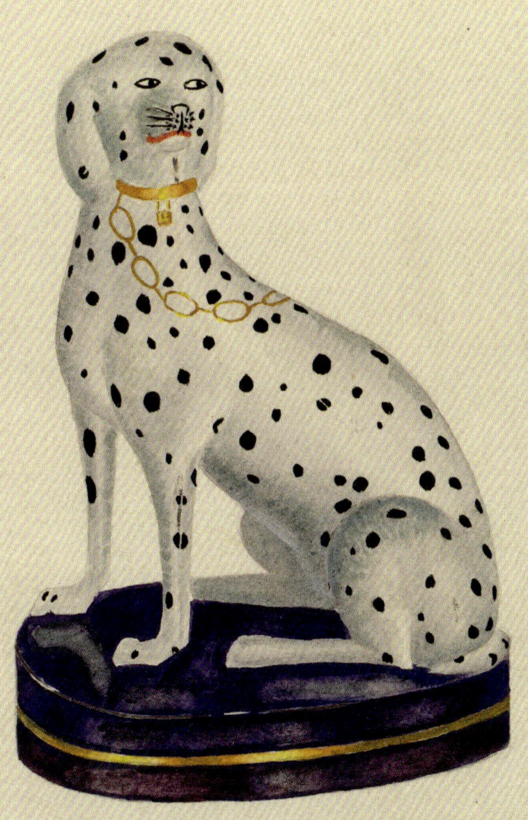

ZOLTON
LUPUS

FIGURE OF A POODLE

British, 1820–1840, earthenware

Staffordshire figures are folk art ceramics made in the industrial area of Staffordshire, England. I cannot emphasize enough the eccentric majesty of every one of these works I have seen, and this poodle is certainly no exception. Incredible. Absolutely unhinged.

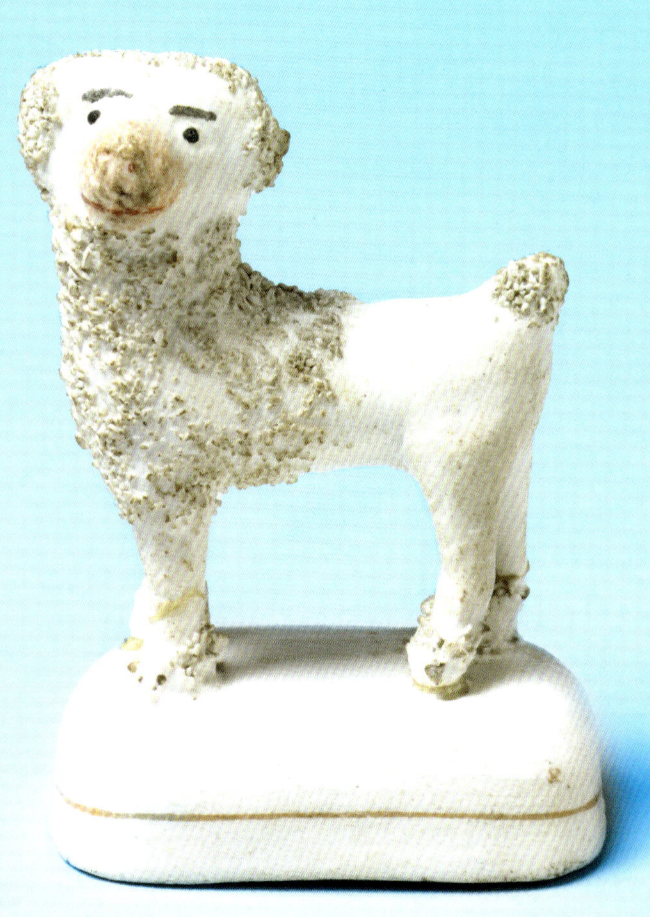

PENDANT

French, 14th century, Champlevé enamel, copper, and gilt

In the fourteenth century, Limoges, where this pendant was made, was famous for its enamel techniques. But, sadly, the industry was destroyed when a villain named Edward the Black Prince stormed in and sacked the town. At least this serene scene of a hound basking in the shade of a flowering tree survived. And we get a happy ending: Limoges's enameling industry was rekindled in the fifteenth century, and the region continues to produce work to this day! Huzzah!

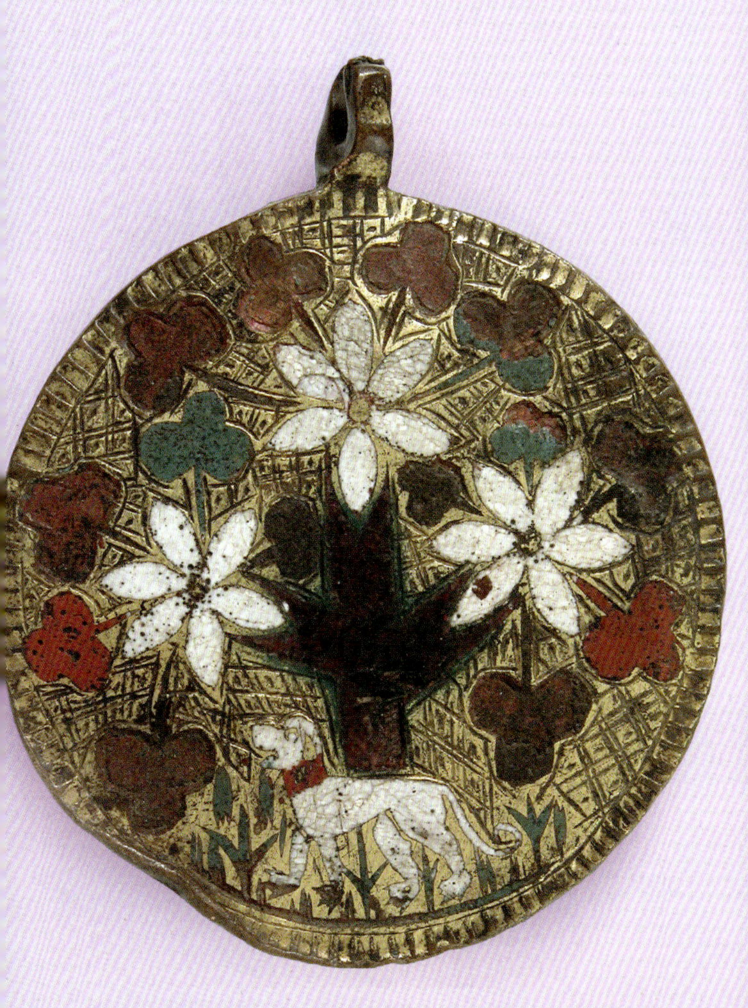

THE PUG LADY

German, 1744–1750, porcelain

In 1738, after Pope Clement XII banned Catholics from being members of the Freemasons, a group of rebellious Germans decided to make up their own secret society, Mops-Orden, or Order of the Pug.

To be initiated into the group and remain a member, you had to

1) Wear a dog collar.
2) Scratch at the door to be let in.
3) Be blindfolded while club members barked at you.
4) Kiss the literal ass of a porcelain pug.
5) Vow to maintain the secrecy of the order.
6) Carry your silver pug medallion at all times.

All that to say, if you saw this statuette—made for Mops-Orden members—in someone's home, you should reach immediately for your silver pug medallion and give a conspiratorial wink.[6]

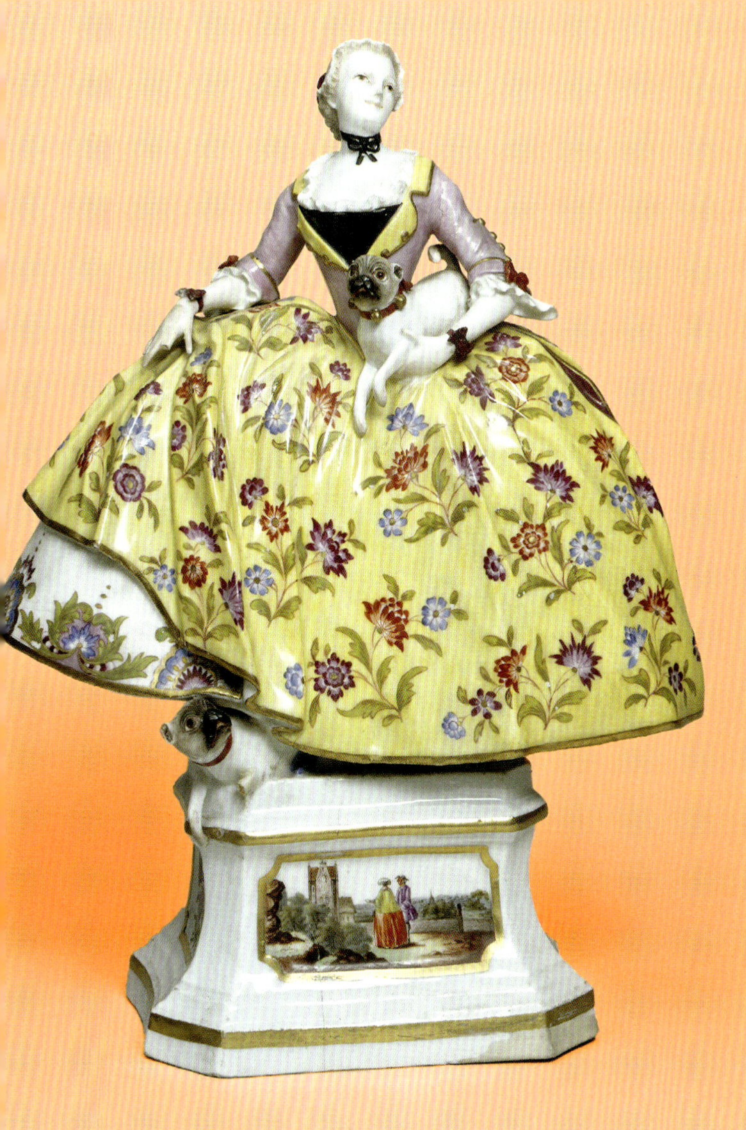

APULIAN DOG HEAD RHYTON

Greek, 340–330 BC, terracotta

Rhytons like this one were typically filled with wine and used both for rituals and for recreational drinking.

But get this:

1) Most rhytons can't be set down without spilling the contents. So, message received: Drink up, and keep on drinking!

2) While taking a sip, the drinker's face was basically replaced by the face of the animal on the rhyton, and that is *funny*.

The ancient Greeks clearly knew how to have a very good time.

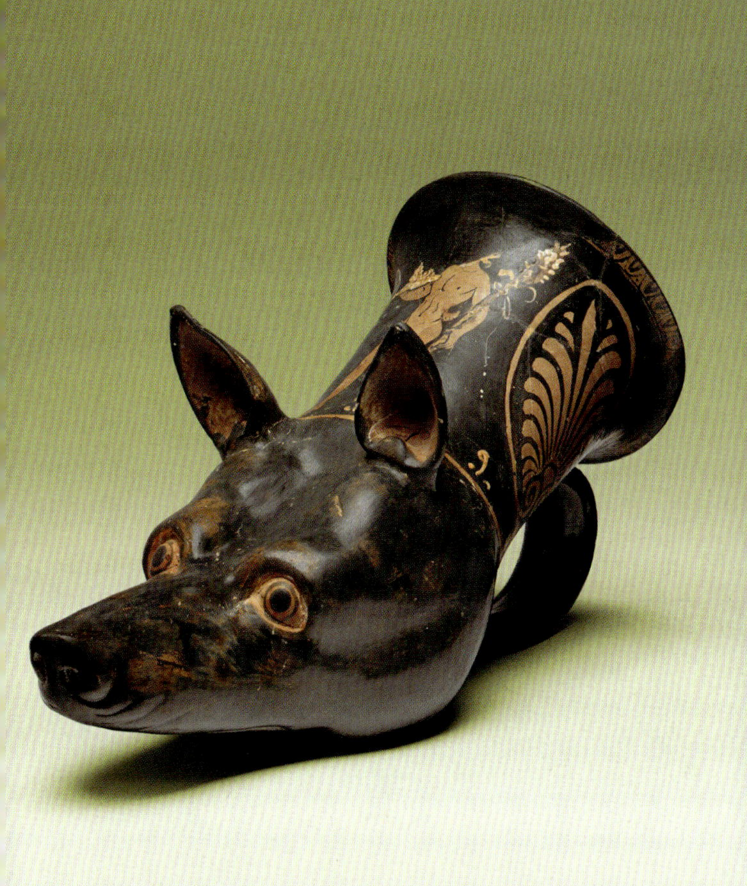

MUSETTE, A MALTESE DOG

Jean-Baptiste Gille, French, 1855–1868, porcelain

Who is Musette the Maltese? And why did the famous French sculptor Albert-Ernest Carrier-Belleuse have a lesser-known sculptor, Jean-Baptiste Gille, execute this work for him?

Was it because he was heartbroken by the death of a beloved dog and couldn't bear to do the sculpting himself? Or was it because a wealthy patron wanted a likeness of their pup and Carrier-Belleuse needed the cash but didn't want to do the work himself, so he commissioned a friend to do it?

I've tried to find out the answer to these questions for us, but alas, the mystery of Musette is here to stay.

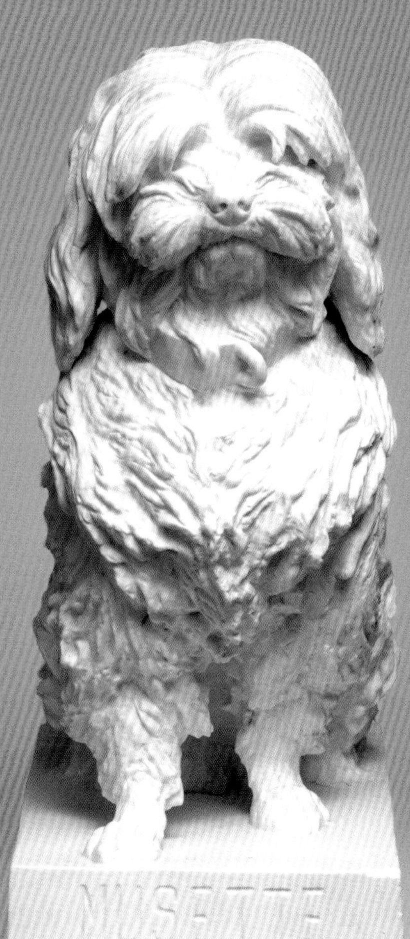
NUSETTE

DOG

Mexican (Colima), 2nd–4th century, clay

Myths about passing from this life to the next are generally fascinating, but the story told by the indigenous people living in Colima, in western Mexico, is especially charming. It goes like this:

To get to the underworld you need to cross a river. To get across the river, you need help from a dog. But not just any dog! White dogs won't be willing to get themselves muddy, so they're out. Black dogs have already been to the underworld and back, so they're exhausted. What you need is a red dog. You'll get a statue of one buried with you, but to make sure your red dog will be there for you when you need them most, you'd better be nice to all red dogs while you're still alive.

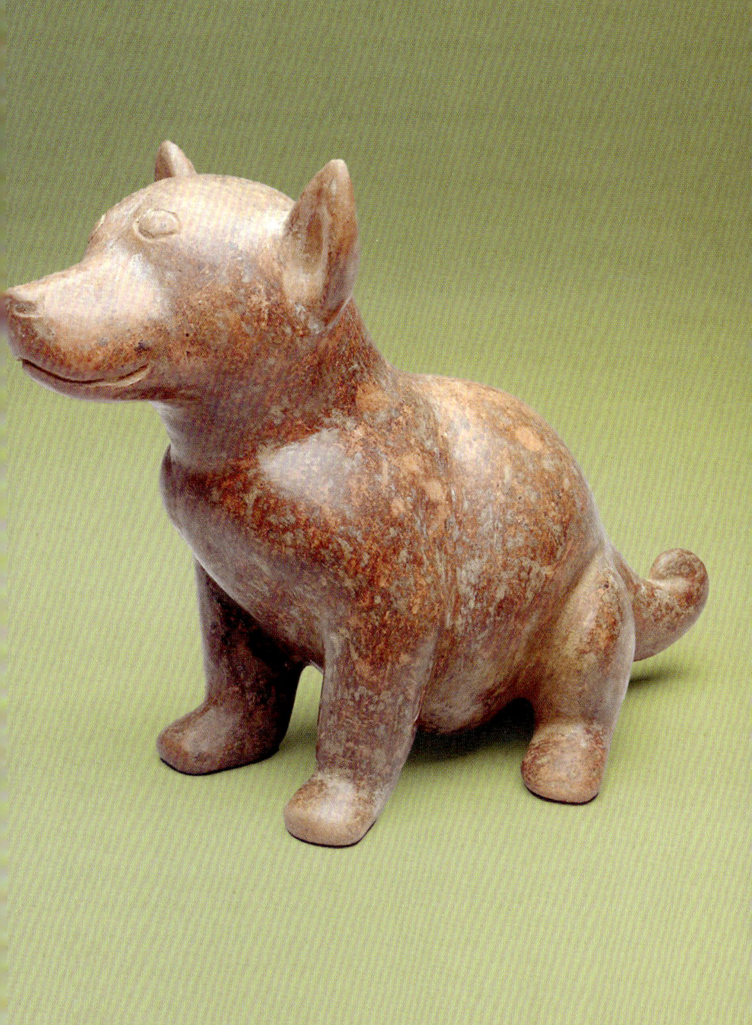

DOGHOUSE

Pieter van Somerwil, Dutch, 1773, silver

Who knew we needed a tiny silver doghouse with a tiny silver dog in it? Yet obviously we do.

For Dutch folks in the eighteenth century, miniature silvers were all the rage. Some wealthy families collected them for their children's dollhouses; others used them as decorations displayed in special curio cabinets.

The creator of this miniature dog and doghouse, Pieter van Somerwil, had three sons. Two became silversmiths, while the third bucked the trend and became a goldsmith. What a rebel.

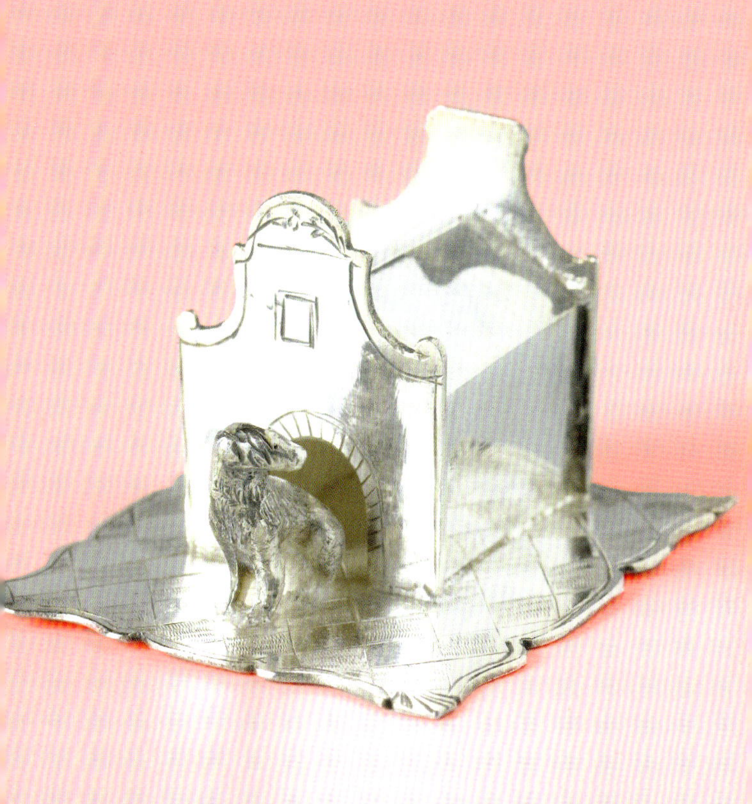

PAIR OF SPANIELS

British (Staffordshire), 1830–1850, earthenware with copper lustre embellishments

Pairs of Staffordshire spaniels were all the rage during Victorian times. The dogs were typically placed on the hearth, both as a decoration and as a sort of amulet for protection.

Some say they were also used as signals for clandestine trysts: One spaniel in the window meant "my husband's away," for example. This makes me think that the Victorians were perhaps not quite as prim and proper as we've been led to believe.

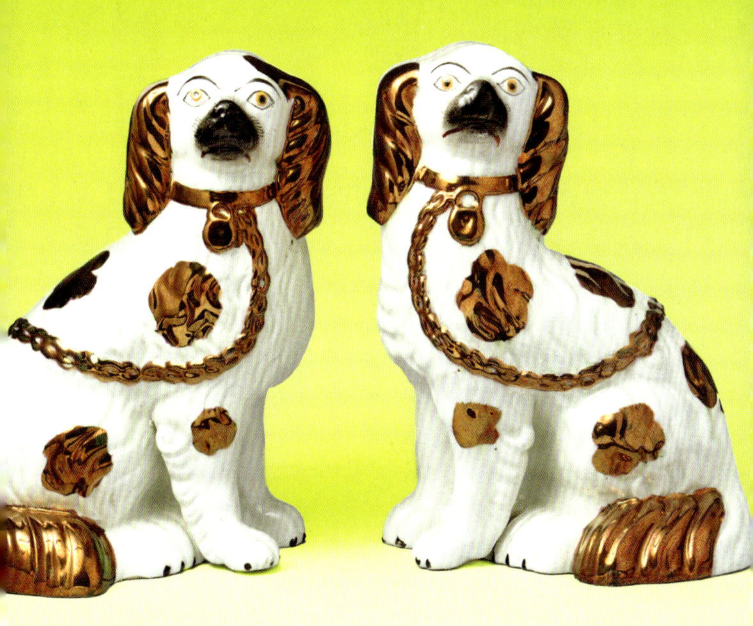

DOG

Franz Anton Bustelli, German, ca. 1760, porcelain

This dog looks like someone just yelled, "Squirrel!"

It's no wonder the face is so expressive: Franz Anton Bustelli, a master sculptor at the renowned Nymphenburg Porcelain Manufactory, was known for capturing comic moments in porcelain. His best-known work was a set of characters from a typical Italian commedia dell'arte—traveling comedy troupes that were essentially live sitcoms with established characters like Joey, Monica, Rachel . . . just kidding. These characters were Harlequin, Harlequina, Pierrot, and others.

I think this pup could hold its own in a comedy troupe any day.[7]

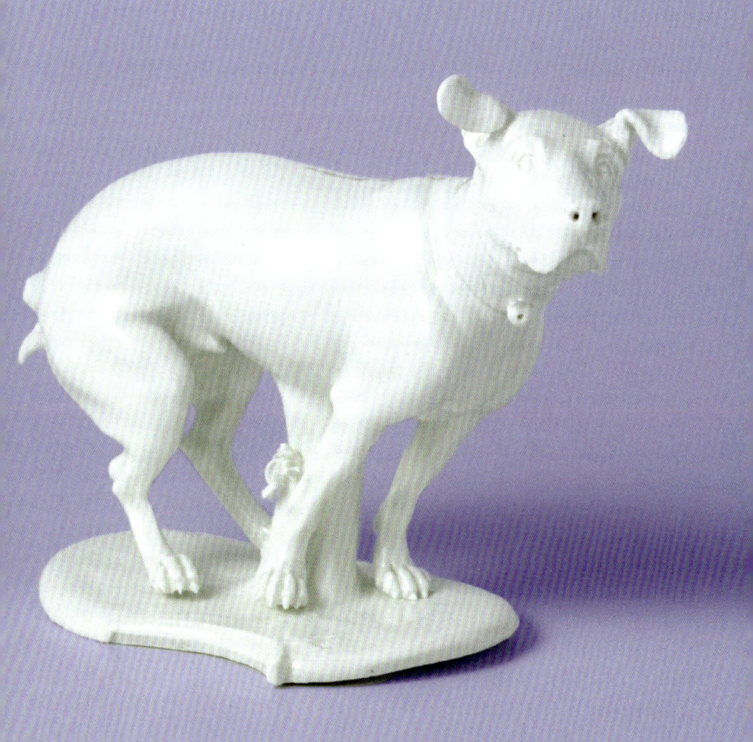

INKSTAND

German, 1530–1550, bronze

An inkstand! The ink goes into a shell! Next to a dog! Whose back has a panel that flips open to hold pens! Why not?!

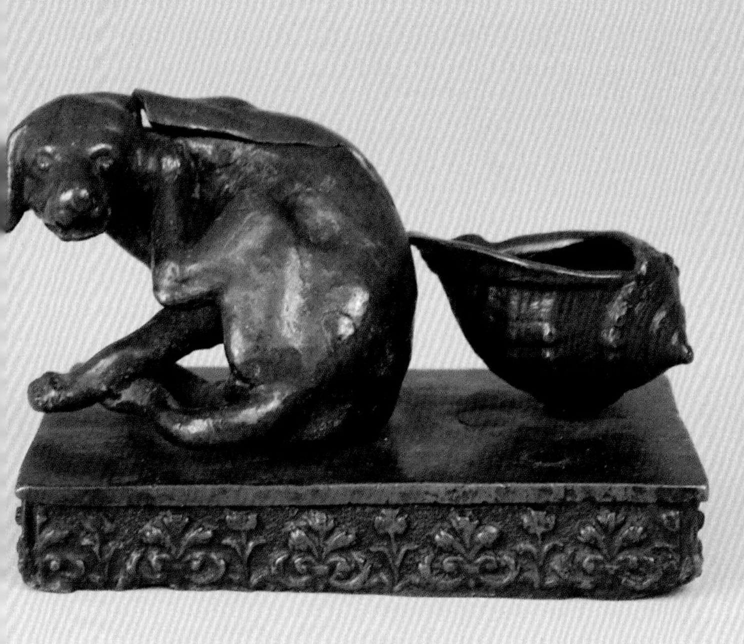

TOY DOG

Egyptian, 1550–1292 BC, ebony

Toys in ancient Egypt? Cuuuuute! There are many depictions of kids playing with toys in Egyptian artifacts: Rattles, balls, and spinning toys seemed to be the most popular playthings.

Ancient Egyptian toys also included several of the kind we see here, featuring an animal's mouth opening and closing when pulled by a string.

Underscoring the importance of toys during the third century BC is a letter (in the form of a papyrus, of course) from a woman named Diogenis to her brother, Aurelius Alexander. She writes that she's moving to a new house soon and that she has completed an errand her brother asked her to do. Then she adds, "Many greetings to little Theon. Eight toys have been brought for him by the woman you told me to greet, and these I have sent you."

It's quite wonderful that some things never change: Kids want toys, and the best aunties send them.[8]

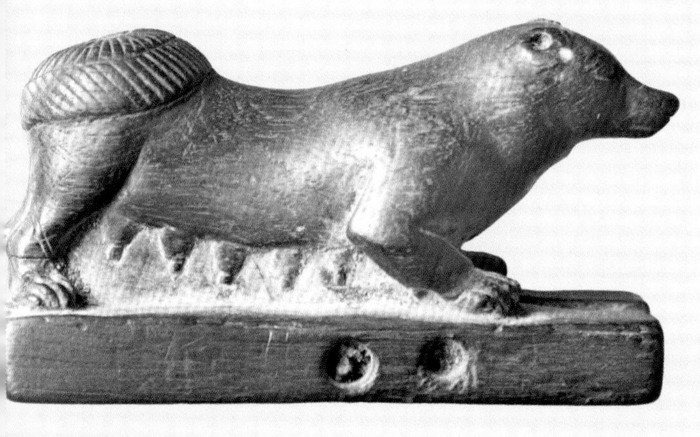

SLEEPING DOG

Paul Wayland Bartlett, American, 1880–1895, plaster

Sculptors Paul Wayland Bartlett and his mentor Emmanuel Frémiet—both part of the "animalier" tradition, which was focused on capturing animals' emotions—would frequently visit the Jardin des Plantes, a botanical garden in Paris where they could spot and sketch birds, squirrels, and sometimes dogs. Back in the studio, they used their sketches to create models for sculptures.

Bartlett eventually swapped his focus from animals to famous historical figures, which include sculptures you can still see at big-deal places like the US Capitol and the Louvre.

That's all fine and good, but I do find myself wishing he'd stuck with his sweet animal pieces. I'm not certain the world needed more sculptures of Benjamin Franklin or the Marquis de Lafayette, but hey, what do I know?[9]

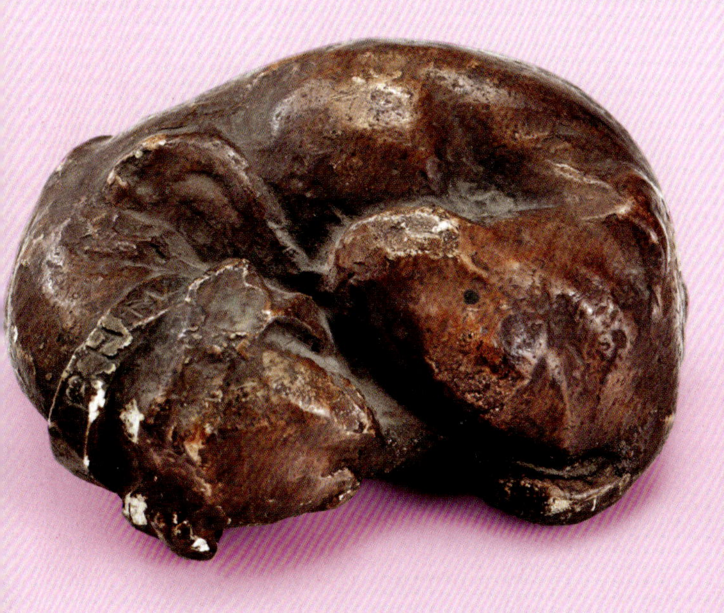

LEAPING DOG

French, 18th century, glass, lampwork

When I dream of being able to ride a giant, beautiful dog, *NeverEnding Story* style (and I do), this is the dog I'm dreaming about.

This piece was made by melting glass onto an iron framework. The French artists who did this work had the most lyrical job title ever: *souffleurs à la lampe*. (It loses a lot of charm when translated to English as "lamp blowers," so let's just stick with the French term, shall we?)

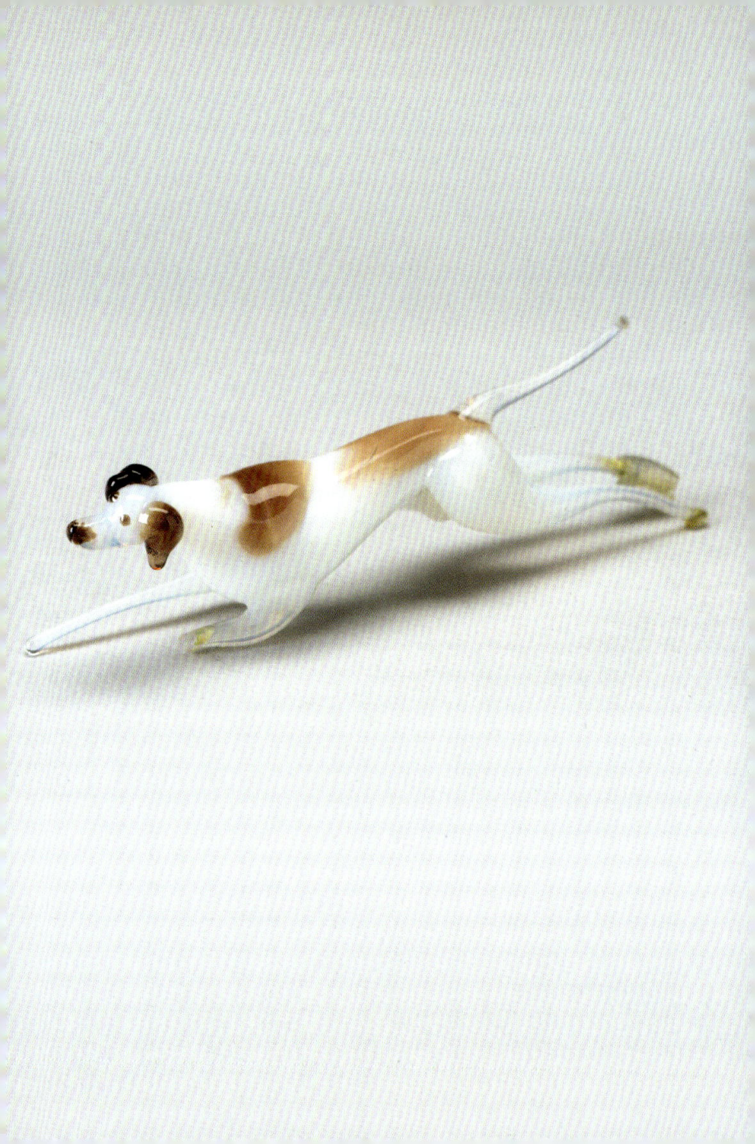

DOGS PLAYING

Mexican (Colima), 200 BC–AD 500, ceramic

Here's a sculpture from ancient Mexico of dogs goofin' around. Other Colima sculptures show dogs wrasslin', hanging out with their friends, sleeping, and more. Not only do these kinds of sculptures suggest that dogs were a cherished and integral part of everyday life, but they also tell us that the Colima culture valued playfulness and humor so much that they were considered subjects worthy of sculpting. I totally agree.[10]

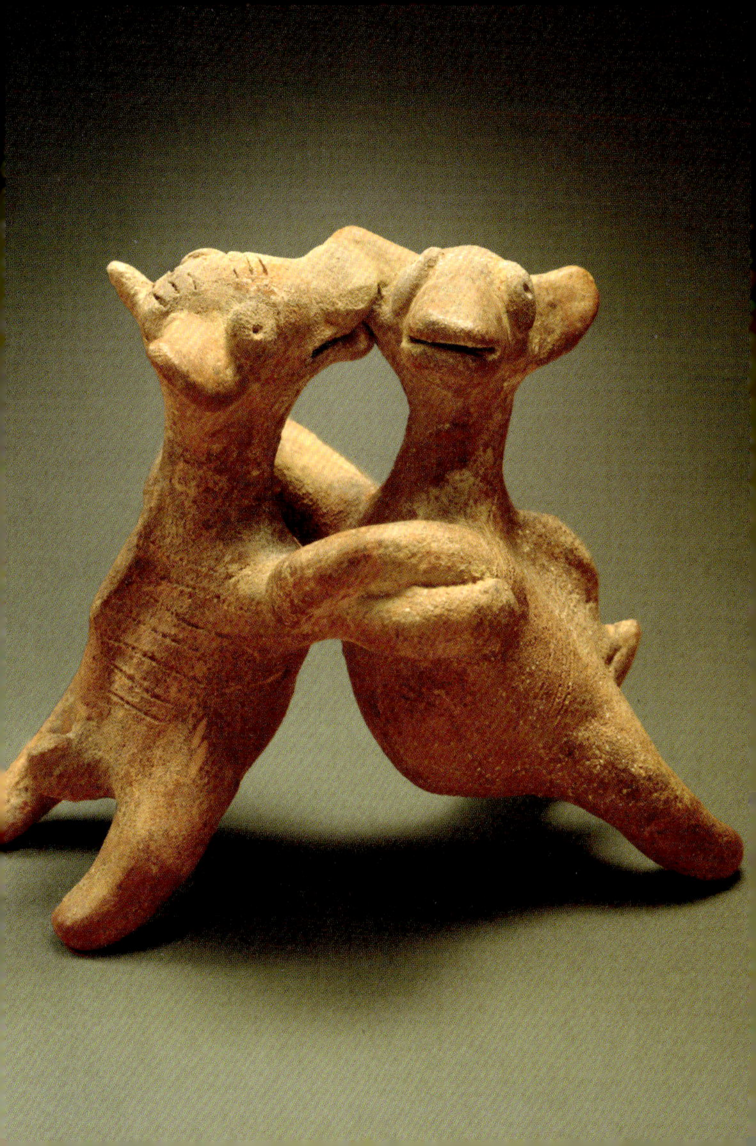

TEXTILE FRAGMENT WITH REPEATING PATTERN OF DOGS ON DOTTED GROUND

Japanese, 18th–19th century, silk

Adorable little dogs with a polka-dot background woven in silk? I would trade all the clothes I own for a new wardrobe made entirely of this fabric.

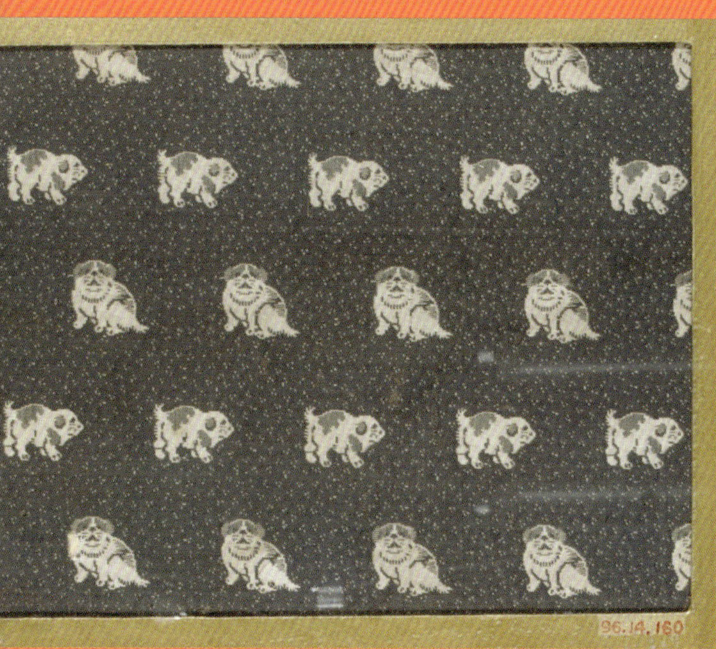
96.14.160

DOG WITH ORANGE BIB

Japanese, 1615–1868, wood, ground shell, silk, and pigments

Question: Why does this dog need a bib?

Follow-up question: When the bib (and the dog) are this cute, do we really need the answer to the first question?

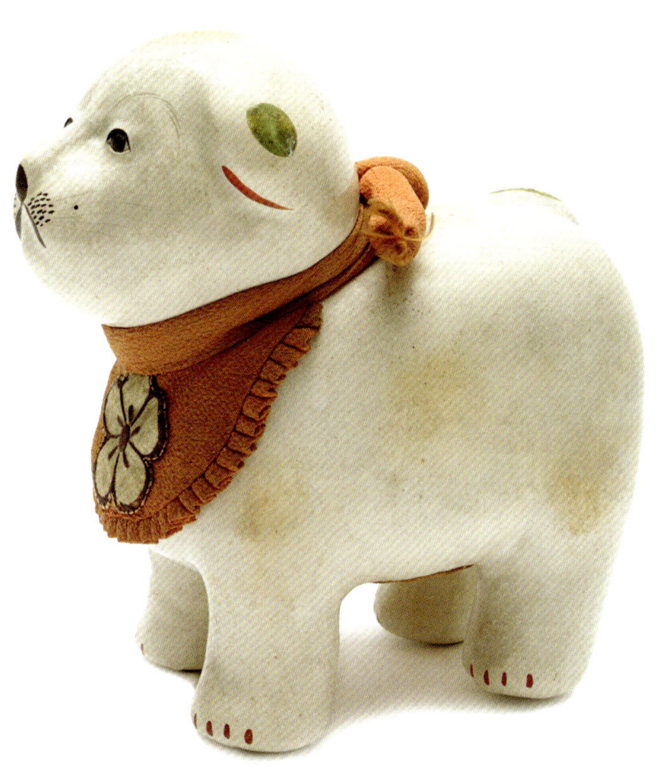

CARVED INTAGLIO GEMSTONE WITH A RUNNING AND BARKING DOG

Roman, 1st–2nd century, carnelian

Talk about practical: This gemstone comes from a ring that was also a seal. Drop some hot wax on a folded piece of paper, press this baby into it, and voilà—you've not only secured the document from prying eyes, you've also signed it, because of course everyone knows what your seal looks like.

The Roman emperor Augustus's seal was a sphinx; he had extras made for his inner circle so they could "sign" documents while he was away. (Apparently us modern folk aren't the only ones who wish we could clone ourselves.)

If I had a personal symbol on a signet ring, a barking dog like this cutie would be as good as any.[11]

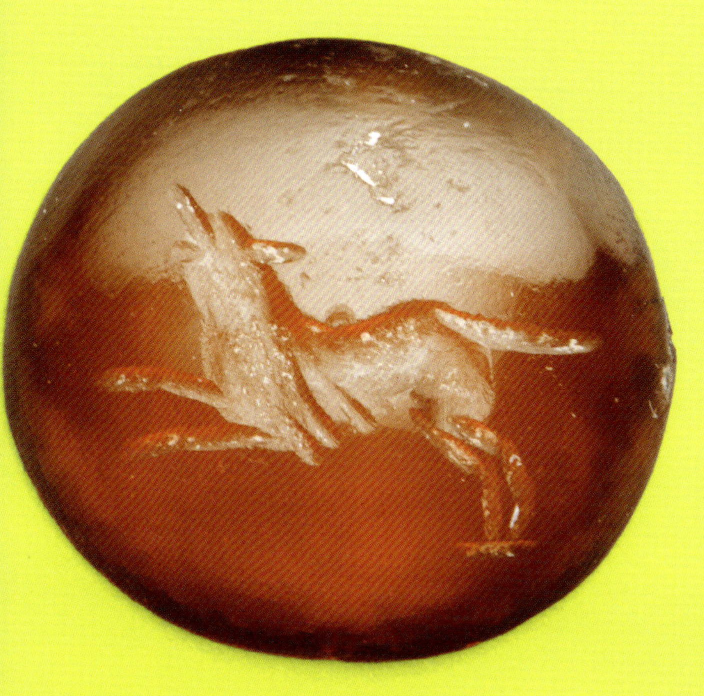

PUPPY

Japanese, 1615–1868, bronze

Things were really popping in Japan during the Edo period (1615–1868), when this piece was made. (Fun fact: The Edo period gets its name from when the Japanese government moved to the city of Edo, now Tokyo.) Things were stable politically and economically, so people had extra cash, brain space, and an appetite for supporting and acquiring arts of all kinds, from Kabuki theater to sculptures like this one.

One characteristic of the Edo period was a preoccupation with making every item in one's environment as beautiful and refined as possible. Mission accomplished with this sleek yet cuddly pup.[12]

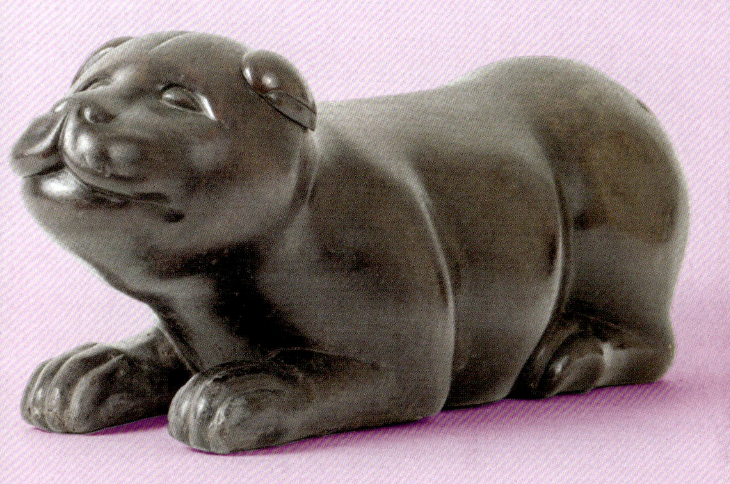

ASKOS IN THE FORM OF A DOG

Greek, 2nd–1st century BC, terracotta

Oil, wine, water: If it was a liquid, you could put it in an *askos*.

The Greeks in the second and first centuries BC went absolutely wild with these vessels, shaping them into all sorts of creatures—some so mysterious archaeologists just call them "zoomorphic."

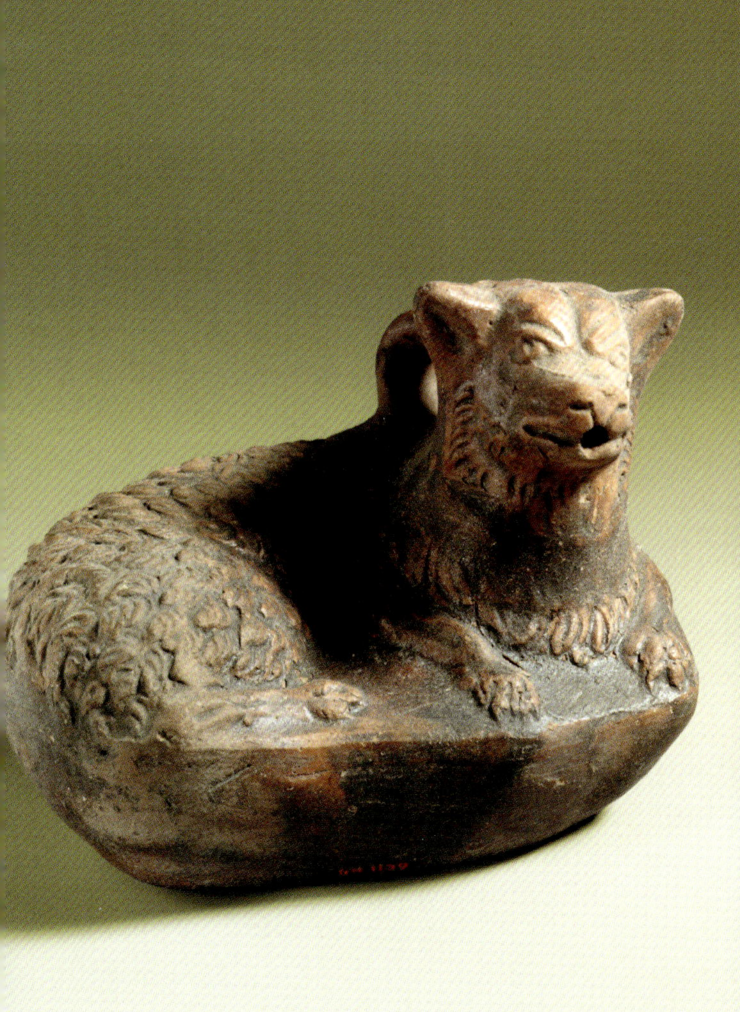

FIGURE OF A DOG

Émile Gallé, French, 1870–1880, earthenware

If you know the artist Émile Gallé at all, it's probably for his incredibly elegant and luminous botanically inspired glass vases—designs that were essential in defining the art nouveau movement.

As it turns out, though, he also made these completely wacky bulldogs.

Most, like this one, are wearing some kind of dressing gown with a floral design. Some have barristers' wigs. Some rock bow ties. One wears a cameo with a picture of a cat on it. Some have collars that include their names—"Mr. Le Baron," for example.

What all of these delightfully bonkers bulldogs have in common are severe underbites and comically deranged looks on their faces.

The lesson I'm taking away: It's not only okay—it's *necessary* to get real silly sometimes.

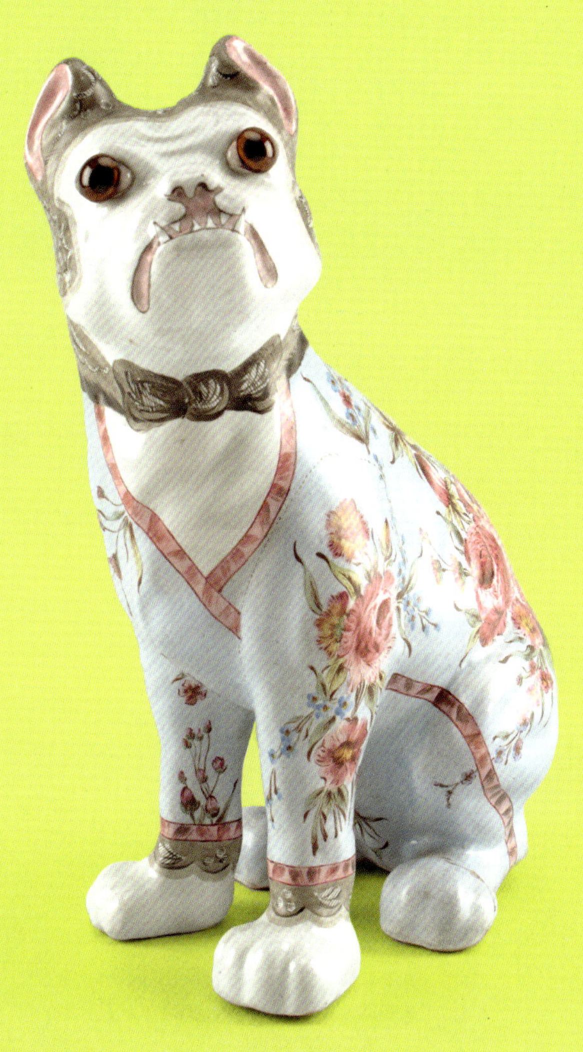

GAME OF HOUNDS AND JACKALS

Egyptian (Middle Kingdom), 1814–1805 BC, carved ebony and ivory

An imagined conversation between an ancient Egyptian and their friend:

Q: What's that?
A: Oh, it's just an ivory playing board shaped like an axe blade propped up on carved animal legs, with a palm tree on top. And ivory game pieces carved to look like jackals and hounds. With a drawer to store the pieces.
Q: What's the game?
A: Basically the same concept as Chutes and Ladders.
Q: Why are you putting it in that tomb?
A: Oh, it's a metaphor. Because what happens in the afterlife is basically like a game of chance.
Q: Okay, cool.
A: Yeah, cool.

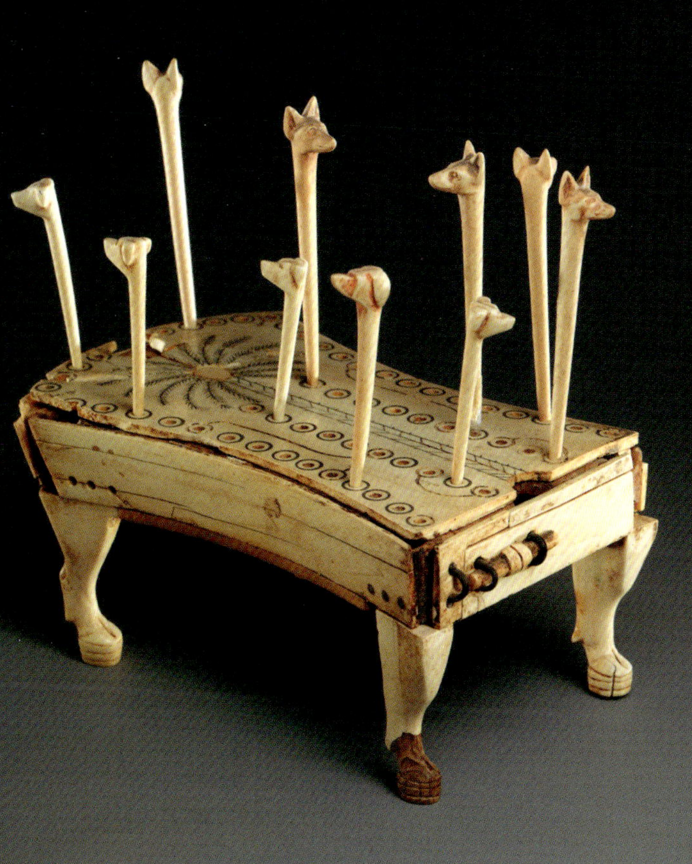

VOTIVE RELIEF

Egyptian, 330–305 BC, limestone

In ancient Egypt, when a family dog passed away, all of the family members would go into mourning. To demonstrate their grief—and tell the world to be extra gentle with them—they would shave all the hair off their bodies, including their eyebrows! They would also sometimes have an effigy made of their beloved friend. We can't know for sure, but perhaps this piece was part of such a commission.[13]

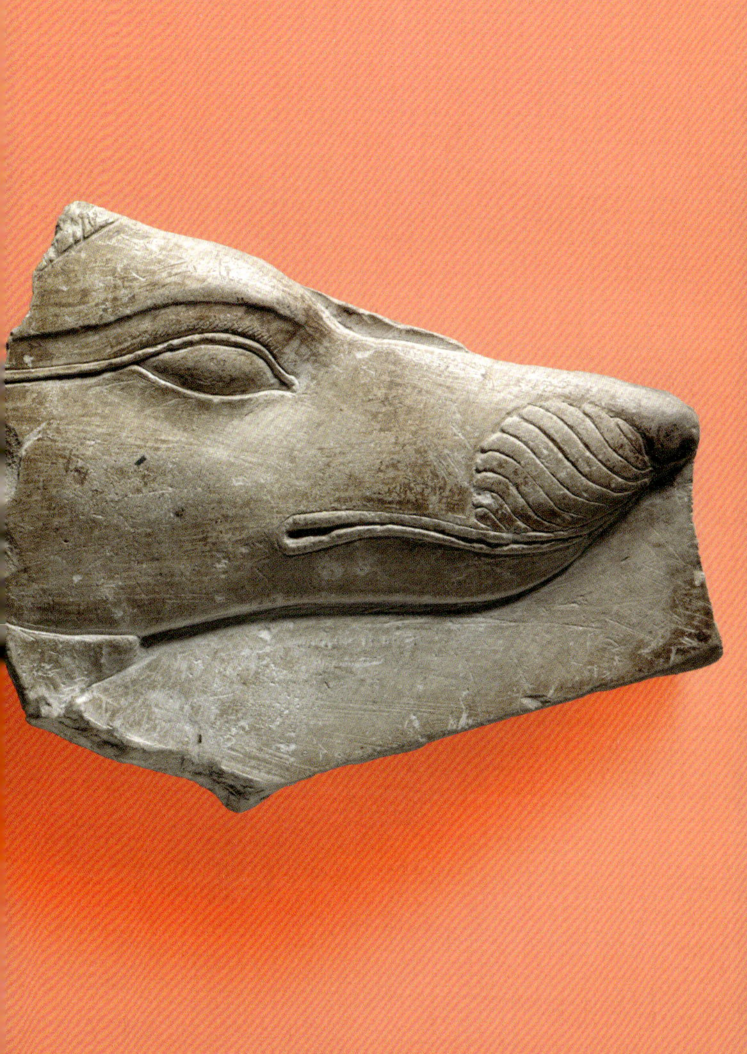

DOG

Italian, 1590–1610, majolica (tin-glazed earthenware)

During the Italian Renaissance, the period in which this platter was created, there was an entire class of objects referred to as *coppe amatorie*, or "love dishes." These dishes featured a beautiful woman in the center, along with a word like *bella* (beautiful), or *unica* (unique), and then lots of filigrees and flowers radiating out around her.

Who's to say this is not a love dish for a dog?[14]

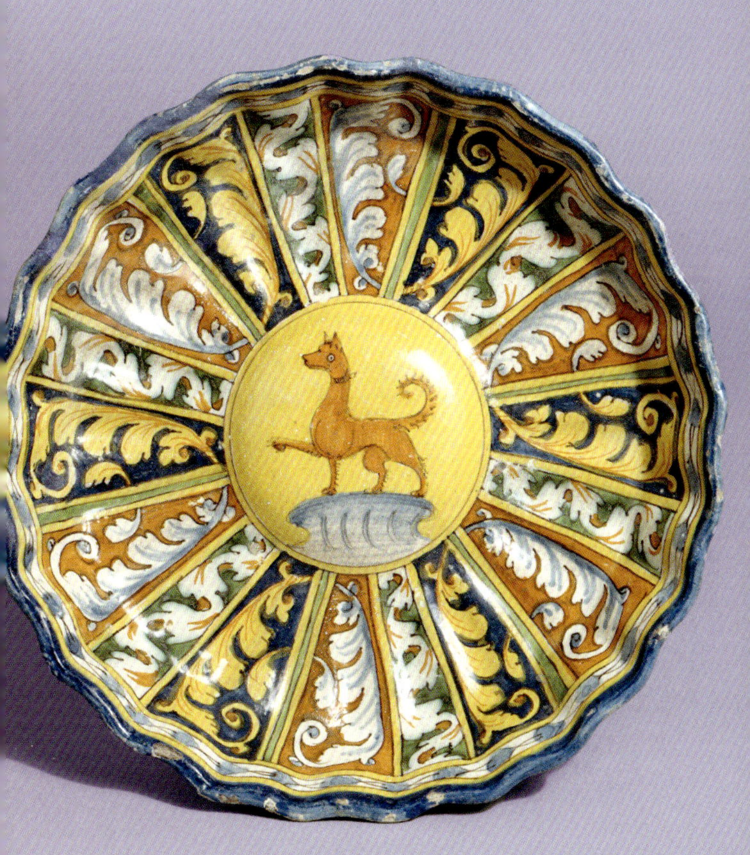

DOG

Greek, 500–475 BC, terracotta

One description says this ancient Greek hound is carrying her pup; another says she's carrying her prey. I choose pup because I am a glass-half-cute kind of person.

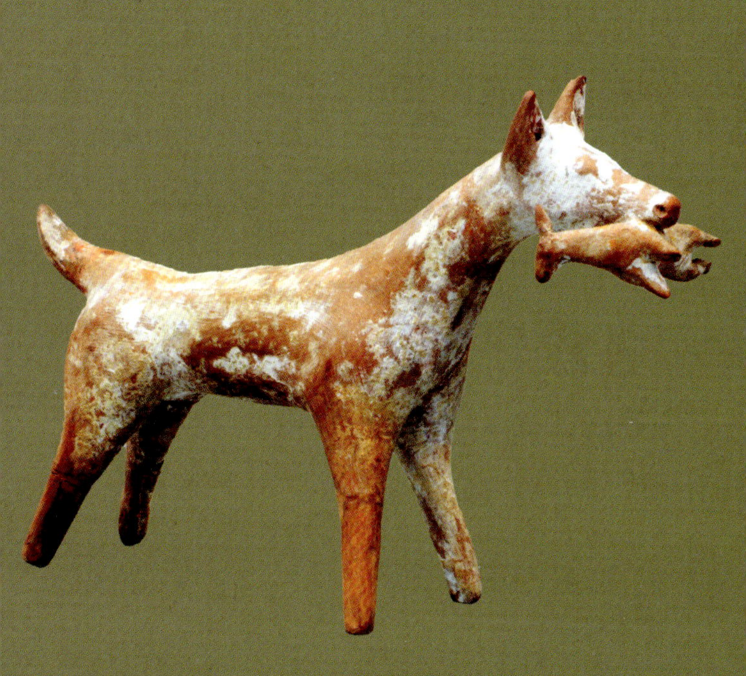

RING

Sicilian, 4th century BC, silver

Museum curators have identified the figures on this ring as a dog and a star. That made me curious: Would fourth-century Sicilians have known about Sirius, the Dog Star?

Turns out they very much did. Sirius rises late in the summer, around the time a heat wave might hit, and it was believed to have the power to wreak all kinds of havoc, from killing crops to causing fevers.[15]

In a Groundhog Day kind of way, people believed that if Sirius was shining bright, you could expect cool breezes on the way. If it was dim, prepare for problems.

Appeasing Sirius required prayers and sacrifices that included money and sometimes jewelry. What are the odds that a ring like this one was among the offerings?

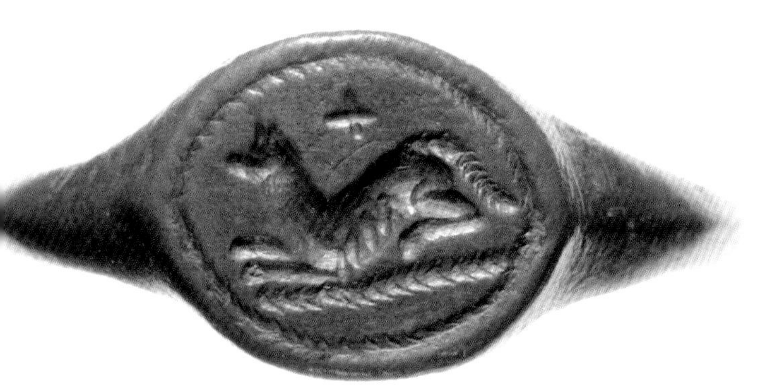

HUNTING DOG SCRATCHING

Attributed to Johann Joachim Kändler, German, 1775, porcelain, Meissen Manufactory

Another banger from the artisans of the Meissen Manufactory, makers of fine porcelain figures.

In the eighteenth century massive dinner parties were a favorite aristocratic activity. The aristocracy went all out on the table decorations, creating whimsical and/or satirical table-length scenes using figurines made of marzipan or sugar.

Meissen executives saw an opportunity: Why not convince people to replace perishable figurines with porcelain equivalents?

Their plan worked, and *Monkey Orchestra*—an opulent and completely ridiculous set of twenty-one monkeys dressed in rococo costumes playing French horns, cellos, flutes, etc.—was born. The first customer? Madame de Pompadour, mistress to King Louis XV.[16]

There isn't a dog equivalent for the *Monkey Orchestra*—yet. Meissen Manufactory is still in operation today, so don't be shy: Make your wishes known!

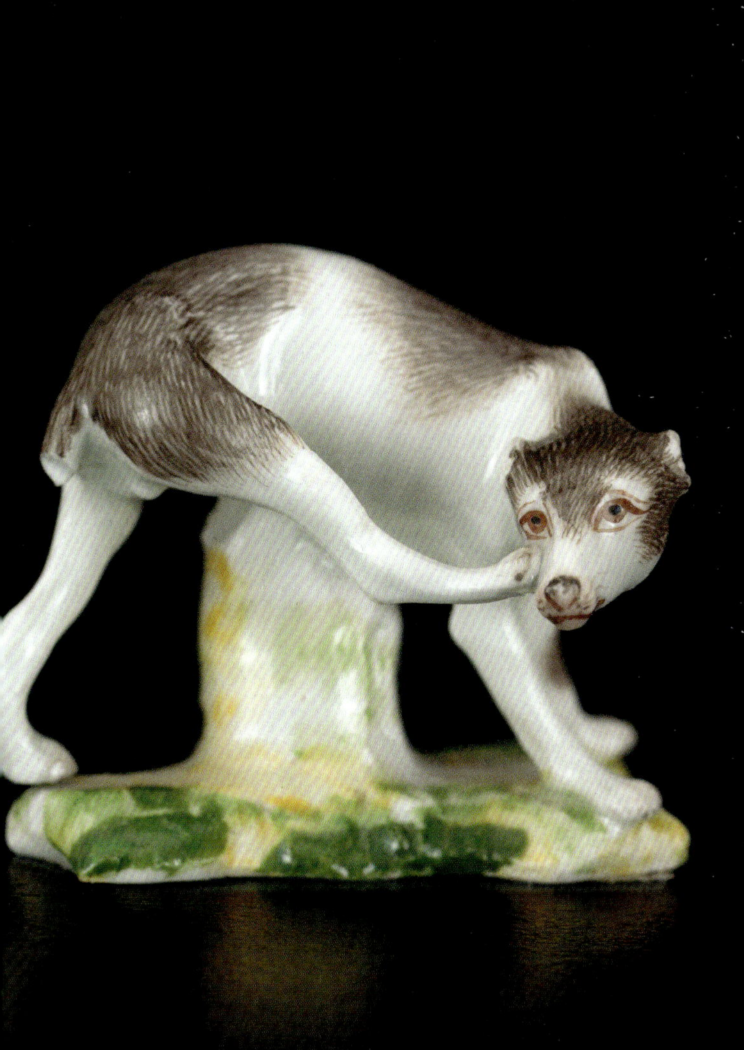

DOG GAME PIECE

Egyptian, 2850 BC, hippopotamus ivory

We have no idea what kind of game this dog was meant to be part of, so let's focus on the adorable collar it's wearing. Archeologists have uncovered a number of dog collars from Ancient Egypt, and many of them had names engraved on them.

Some dogs were named after their positive traits: "Brave One," "Reliable," and "Good Watchman."

Some names were poetic: "Son of the Moon," "Breath of Life," and "The North Wind."

And others . . . well, let's just say the Egyptians (literally) called 'em like they saw 'em: "Useless," "The One with the Bad Temper," and "I Do Not Like." Ouch.[17]

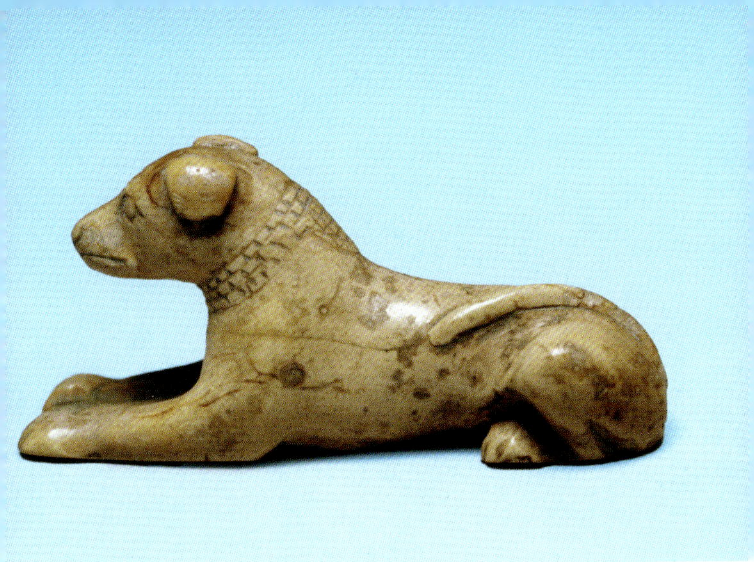

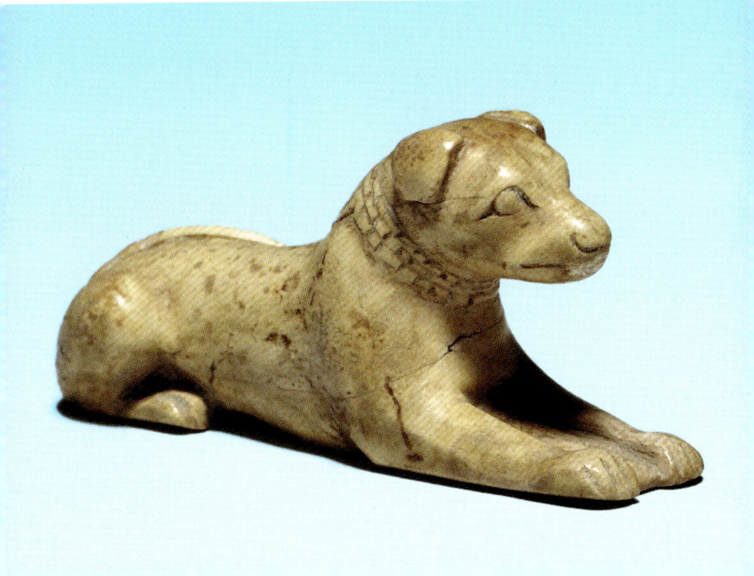

DOG BROOCH

Roman, 1st–2nd century, copper alloy

If this enchanting little Roman brooch were mine, I would name the dog Hortensia, after the first-century BC Roman activist who spoke out against women being taxed to fund a civil war. She said, "Why should we [women] pay taxes when we have no part in the honors, the commands, the statecraft, for which you contend against each other with such harmful results?" Slay, Hortensia, slay![18]

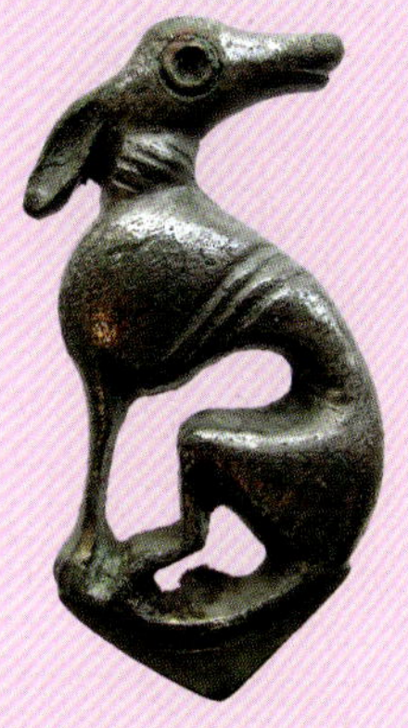

PIPE TAMPERS

British, 1650–1800, copper alloy

Sir Isaac Newton (1642–1727), mathematician, physicist, and formulator of the law of universal gravitation, was being pursued by a young woman who hoped to capture his heart.

As Newton and the woman were holding hands and talking, according to one biographer, "he absentmindedly used her little finger as a tamp for his pipe. Aroused by her sudden exclamation of pain from the heat of the embers in place of the pleasure that should have come from the warmth of love, Newton exclaimed, 'Ah my dear Madam, I beg your pardon! I see it will not do! I see, I see that I am doomed to remain a bachelor.'"

The moral of the story is this: If you need to smush your pipe tobacco down (and you definitely do), get yourself a pipe tamper. It might as well be shaped like a dog.[19]

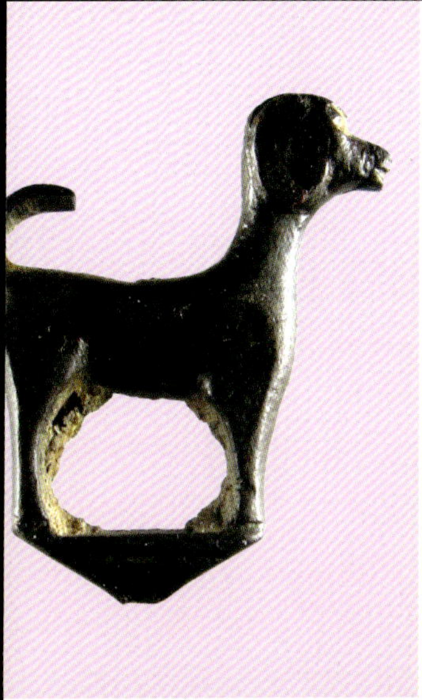

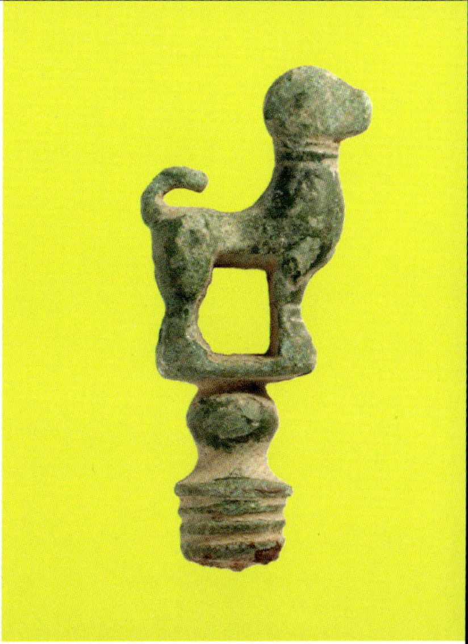

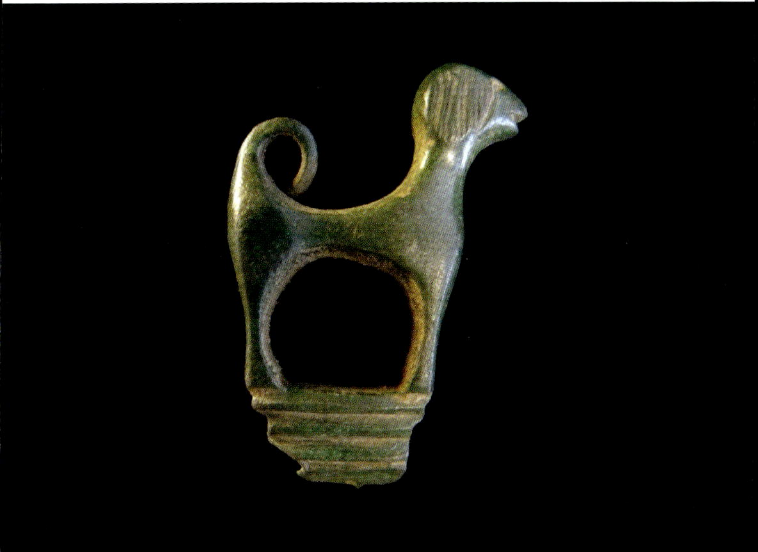

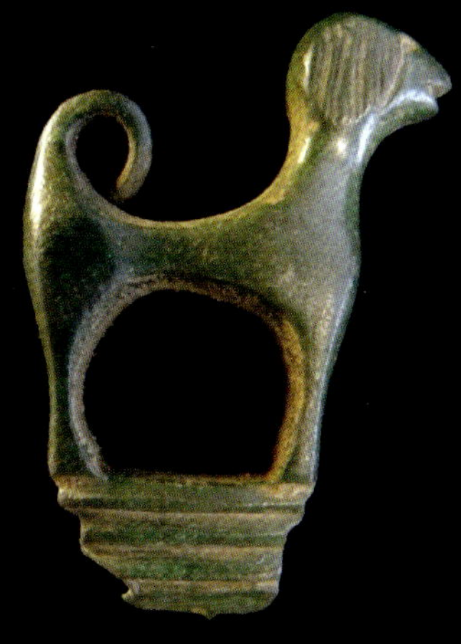

INCENSE BURNER IN THE FORM OF A DOG
(front and back)
Japanese, 1750–1800, porcelain

Three items to consider:

1) This is a freaking incense burner! Delightful scents would be wafting through this pup's mouth and ears!

2) Baby got back. (Which is to say, baby's got a gorgeously rendered koi fish on her back.)

3) Breaking out a rare kind of incense to burn would have been similar to opening a $300,000 bottle of wine from Château Lafite Rothschild: a massive splurge and an unforgettable experience.[20]

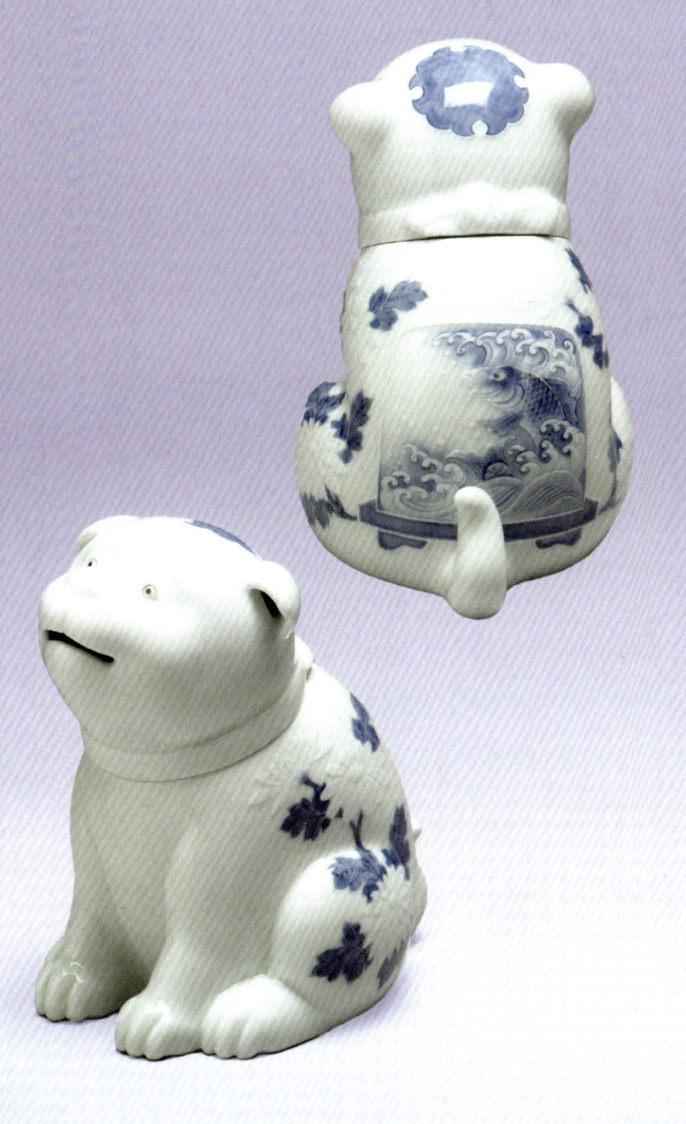

SCARAB GEMSTONE WITH CARVING OF A DOG IN GLOBOLO STYLE

Etruscan, 4th–3rd century BC, carnelian

What a word: *globolo*. As in globular. It's basically a super-fun onomatopoeia.

Globolo carvings were achieved by using rounded drill bits of different sizes to create circles representing, in this case, the head, nose, knees, elbows, and feet of the dog, then carving straight lines to connect the circles together. I love the atomic structure vibe.

Two-sided gemstones like this one (the back has a simple carving of a scarab beetle) also functioned as seals. All you had to do was create a mounting that accommodated two sides. For rings, a rod went through the middle of the gemstone so that it could be flipped over. The mullet of rings, if you will: Business in the front, party in the back![21]

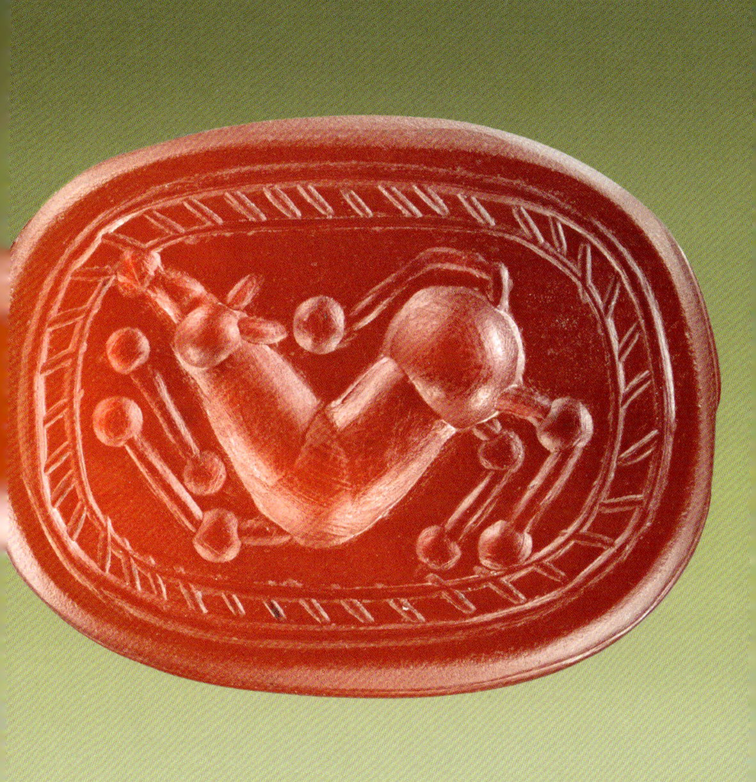

JOINED DOGS

Mexican (Nayarit), 200 BC–AD 500, ceramic

These pups might be giving conjoined twin vibes, but the connection is symbolic rather than literal: This may be a depiction of littermates.

Other joined figures found in the Nayarit region are thought to represent links between ancestors, family members, a shaman and their patient, or a married couple. Given how sweet this sculpture is, I'd say two heads are definitely better than one. (I can hear you groaning, and you're not wrong.)[22]

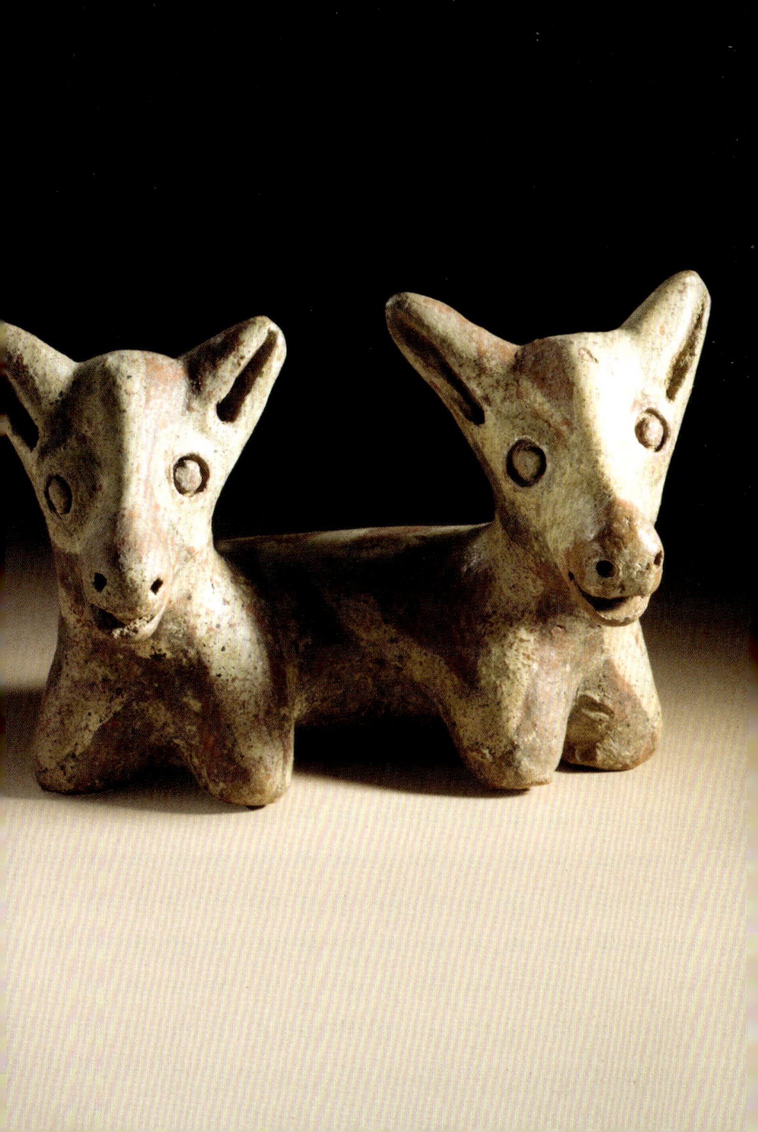

DOG

Chinese, 902–979, sandstone and celadon

I would like this dog to be my best friend forever. And luckily, that's exactly what he was made for.

This pup is a mingqi, a spirit object. In eighth-century China humans were believed to have two souls. The hun, or spirit soul, ascended to heaven, while the po, or animal soul, stayed with the body and continued living in the realm of the dead.

To ensure a fantastic life after death, tombs would include mingqi representing everything a po needed for comfort, protection, and entertainment, including necessities like servants, musicians, houses, horses, and, of course, their beloved canine companions.[23]

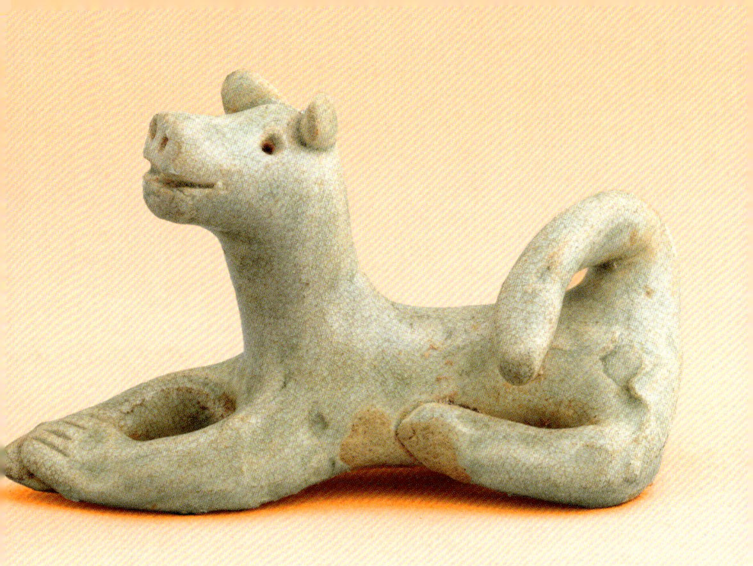

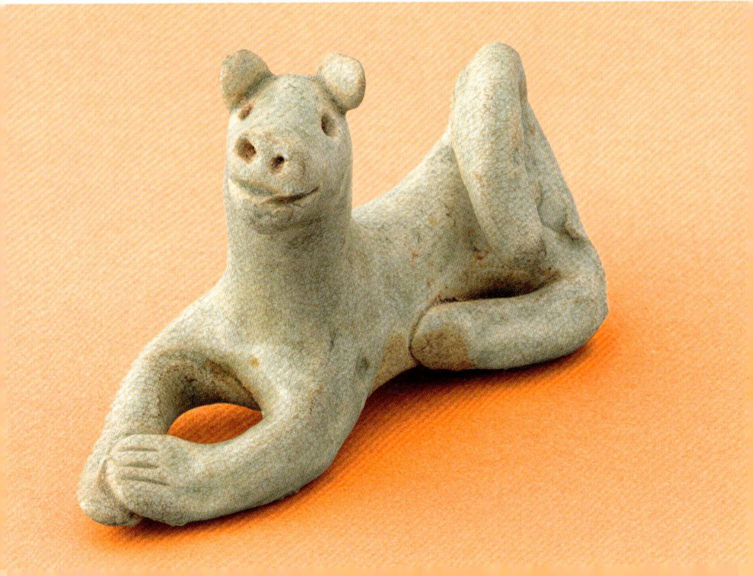

NETSUKE OF SEATED PUPPY WITH SHORT CURLED TAIL

Japanese, mid-19th century, wood and gold lacquer

You wouldn't think that a round little puppy figurine could somehow be elegant, but here we are.

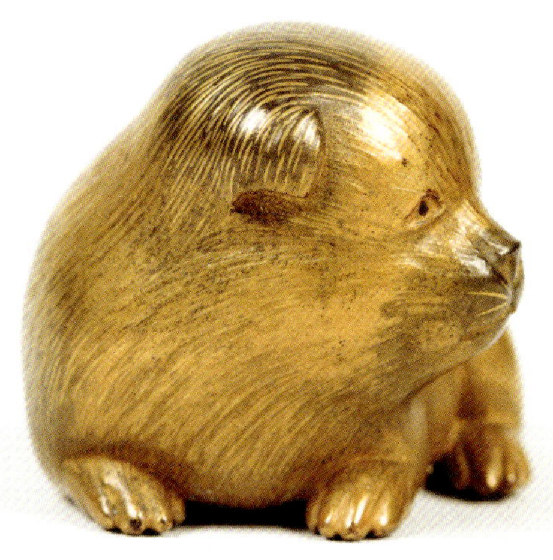

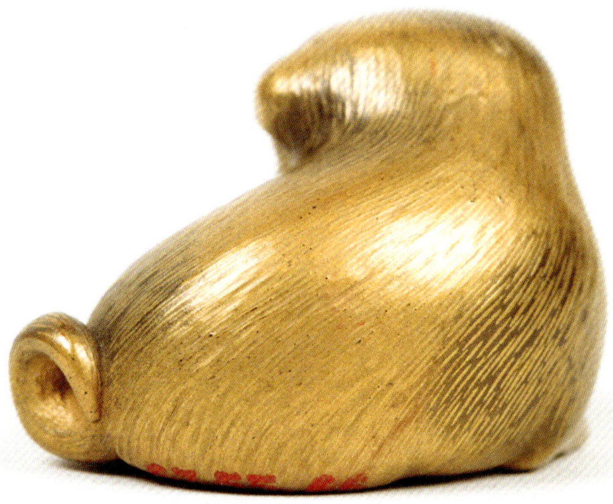

FIGURE OF A RECUMBENT DOG

Chinese, 6th century, gray earthenware with red polychrome

Doesn't this dog look like he should have his own cartoon series? I would definitely follow his adventures, which—since he probably served as a guard in or around a tomb—would probably center on capers with all of his goofy ghost friends.

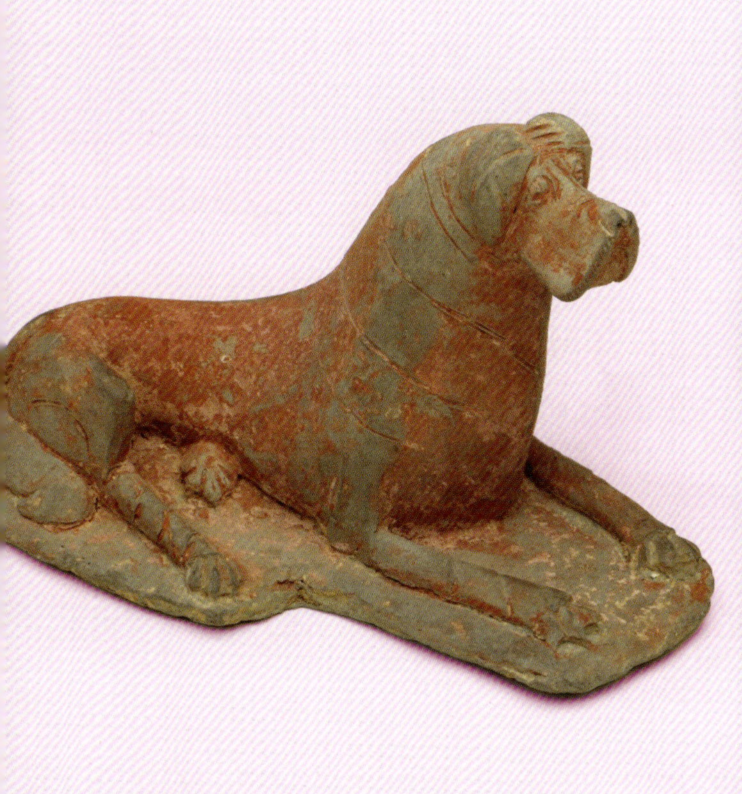

DOG RESTING UPON A COUCH

Edwin Landseer, British, 1817, pencil on paper

Artist Edwin Landseer was beloved during the Victorian era for his drawings, paintings, and sculptures of animals; his most famous pieces are the four bronze sculptures of lions at the base of Nelson's Column in London's Trafalgar Square. A child prodigy, Landseer started drawing astonishing pictures of animals when he was five years old. This fluffy white Pomeranian, so sweetly and delicately rendered, was made at the ripe old age of fifteen.

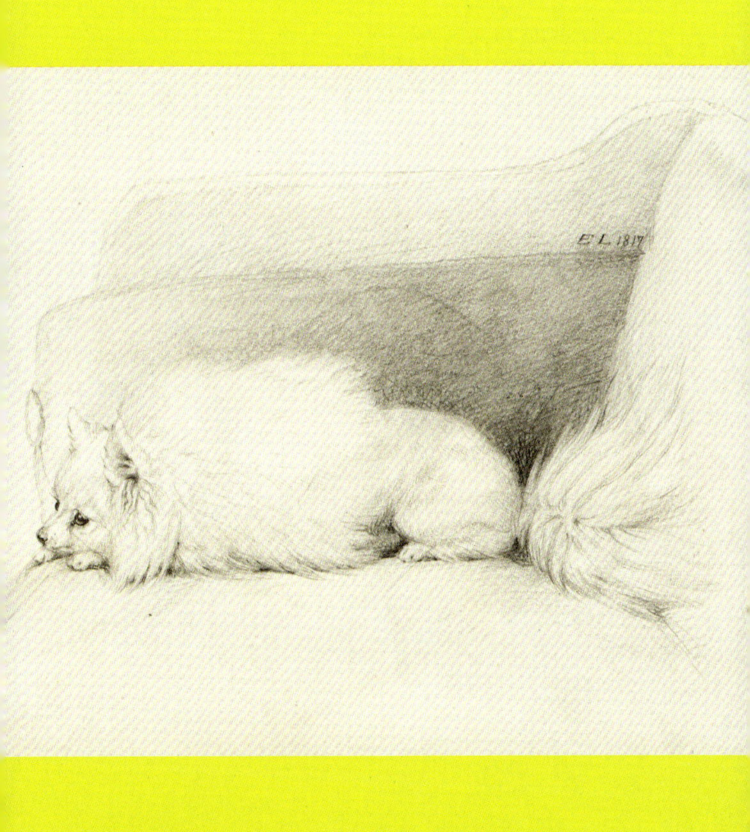
E L 1817

BROOCH
(front and back)
Roman, AD 75–199, copper alloy

Would buy, would wear.

Ancient Romans used brooches in place of zippers, buttons, and Velcro—none of which they had—to hold their clothing together.

Brooches like this one may have originally been enameled and would have been quite colorful. You know, to add a little bling to those blah togas.[24]

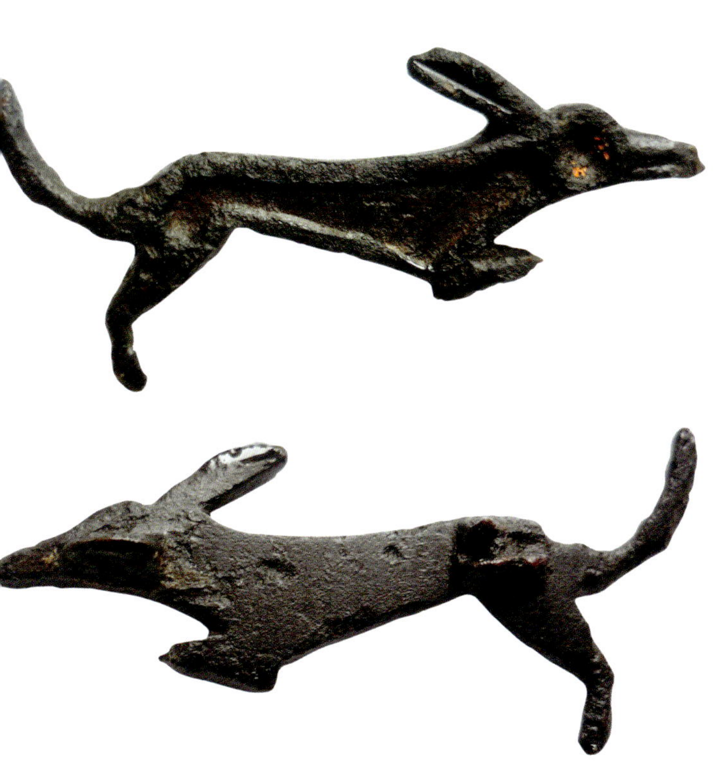

SEATED DOG

Chinese, 4th–6th century, earthenware

This dog kind of looks like a frog, and I'm loving it. Very little is known about this pup, so let's take this moment to reflect on a saying attributed to the Chinese philosopher Confucius: "Knowing something is not as good as liking it. Liking something is not as good as rejoicing in it."[25]

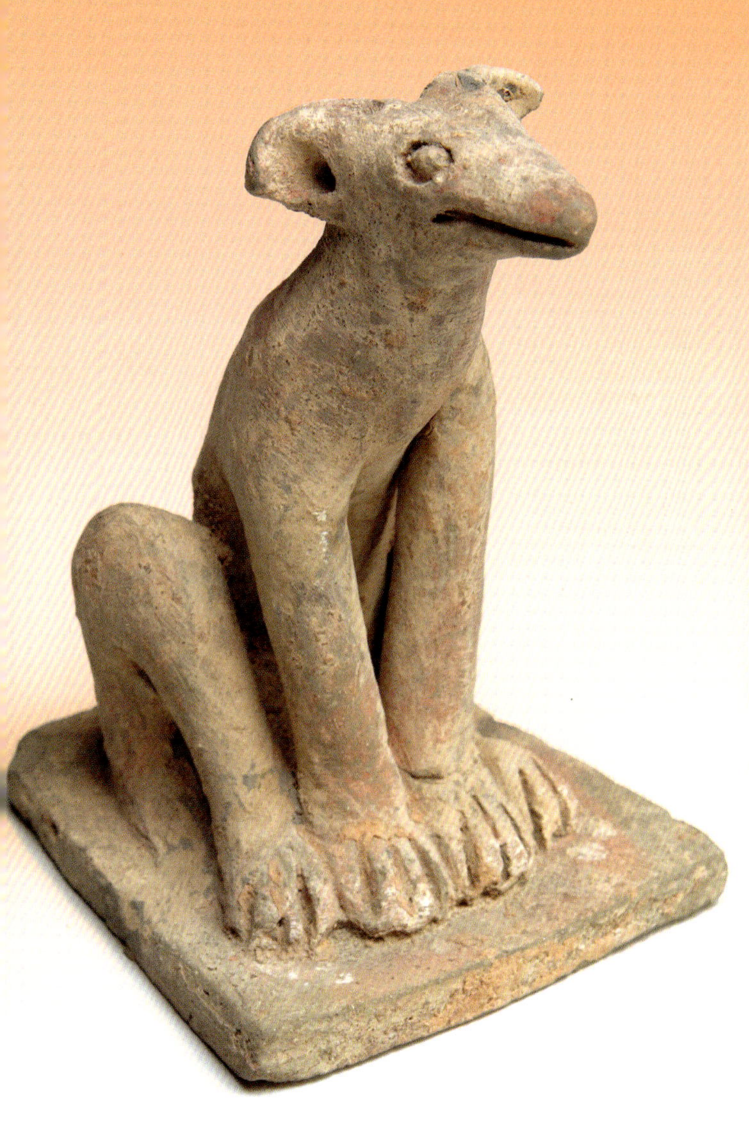

LAMP

Roman, 1st–4th century, terracotta

An oil lamp, but make it adorable.

Oil lamps were everywhere in the Roman empire during the first to fourth centuries. Some of them were downright wacky: A portly nude god holds a bowl at his waist with the wick (wink, wink) inside the bowl. A pair of feet wearing flip-flops with the wick between the two big toes. I could go on.

Not only used to see in homes after dark, oil lamps lit gladiator shows, temples, shrines, and businesses that wanted everyone to know they were open at all hours. They were also given to guests to light their way home after a rager.

Maybe this lamp was the one everybody used when the puppy had to go out in the middle of the night?[26]

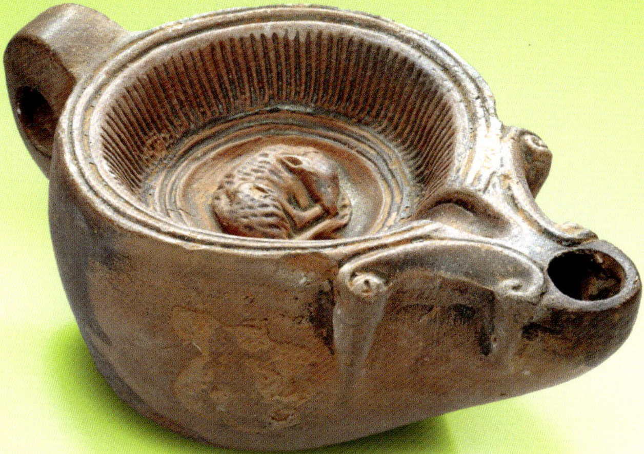

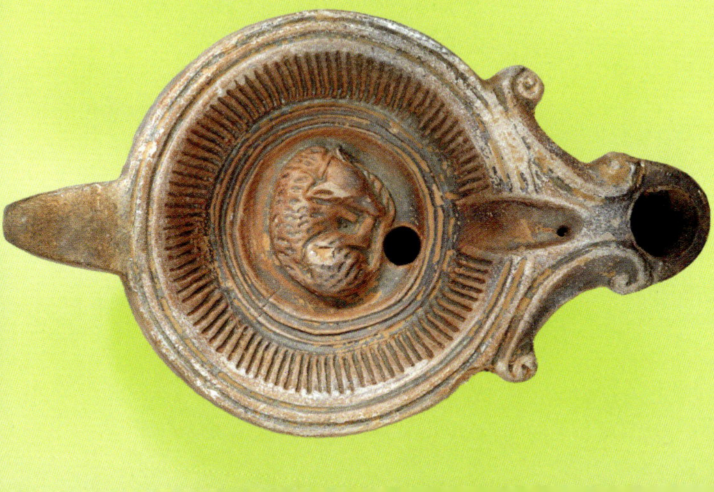

PUG DOGS

German, 18th century, porcelain, Meissen Manufactory

These German pugs definitely look like they're in cahoots. Maybe you were about to eat a giant salted soft pretzel. You left for *one second* and came back to find these two playing tug-of-war with it. They freeze when they see you and give you this look. And of course you forgive them because they are too darn cute to be mad at for long.

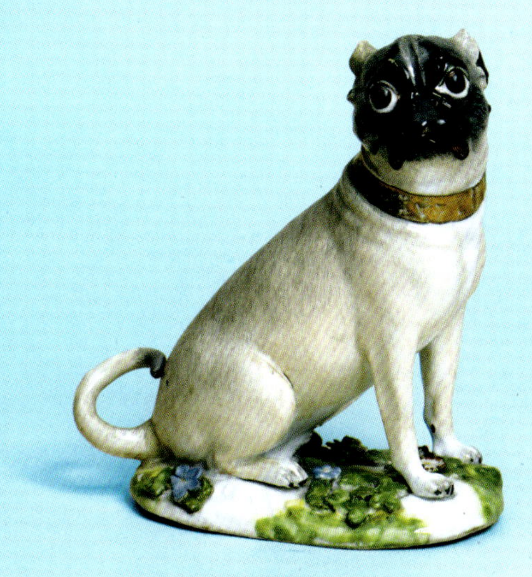

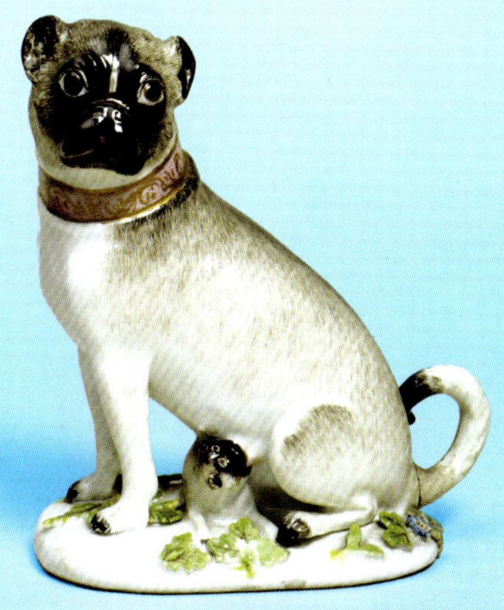

LIMESTONE DOG

Cypriot, 4th–3rd century BC, limestone

Anytime I'm at a museum that has Greek antiquities, I head straight for the Cypriot section. The vibe of things made in Cyprus has been described by one scholar as "exuberant," and I totally agree.

Cypriot artisans typically portrayed dogs alongside deities like Artemis, goddess of the hunt, but this huggable buddy stands on its own, indicating that it may have been protecting a tomb. Have you ever seen a sweeter-looking tomb guard? I bet you have not.[27]

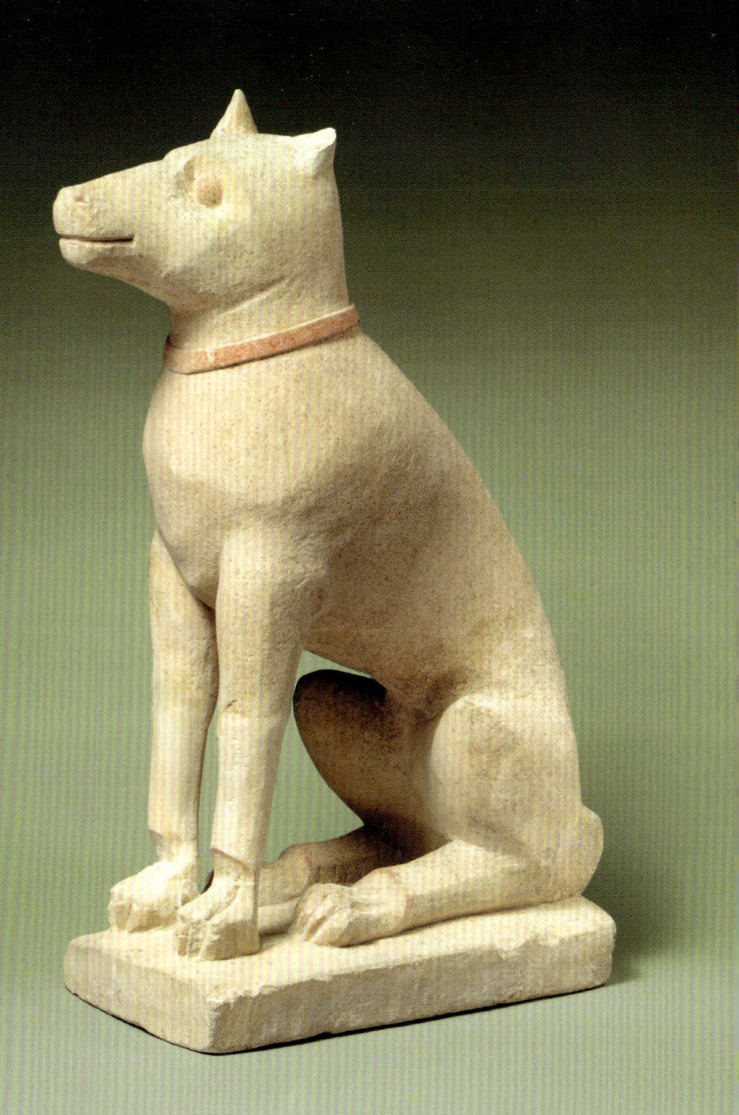

WATERSPOUT FRAGMENT IN THE SHAPE OF A DOG

Roman, 1st century BC, terracotta

This waterspout in the shape of a dog prompts a question: Why shouldn't all elements of public infrastructure be this cute? We have the technology! If you know someone with the power to make this happen, please convince them to do so.

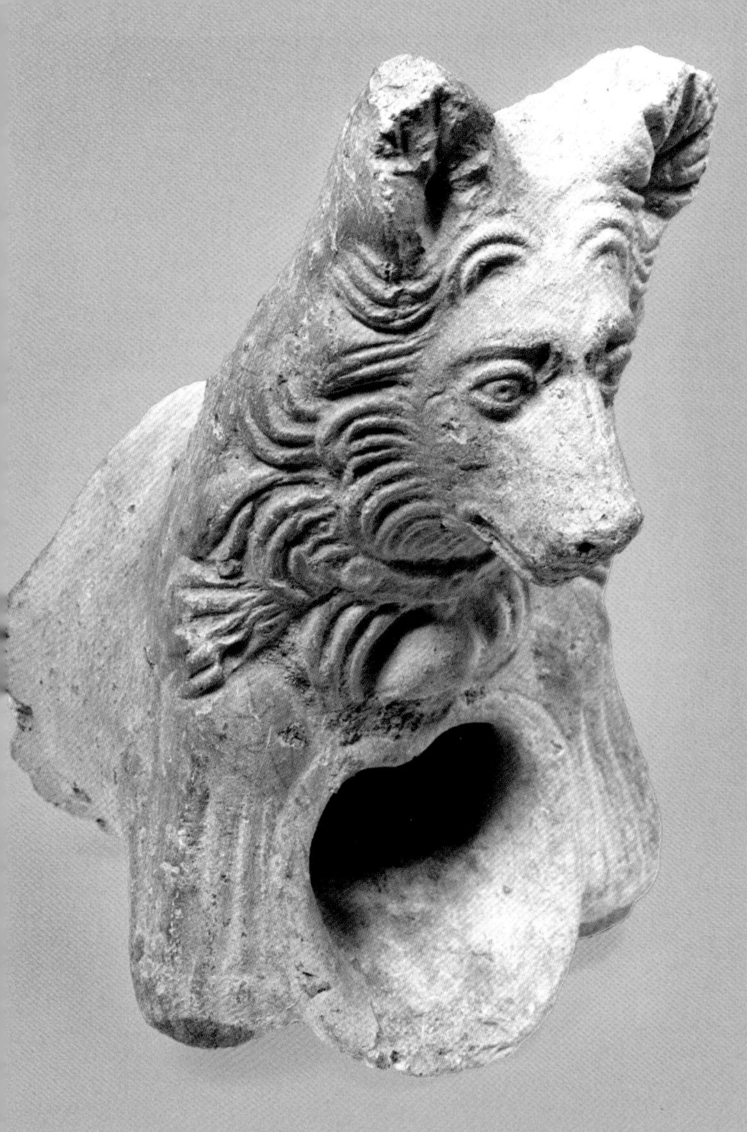

DOG

Taiwanese (Yuan Dynasty), 1271–1368, jade

Jade is an incredibly important material in Asia—both practically and spiritually. Rather than being made with the more common green hue, this piece was beautifully carved in white jade that contains ochre spots. Which is perfect, because that means the dog's little cinnamon bun tail is the appropriate color.

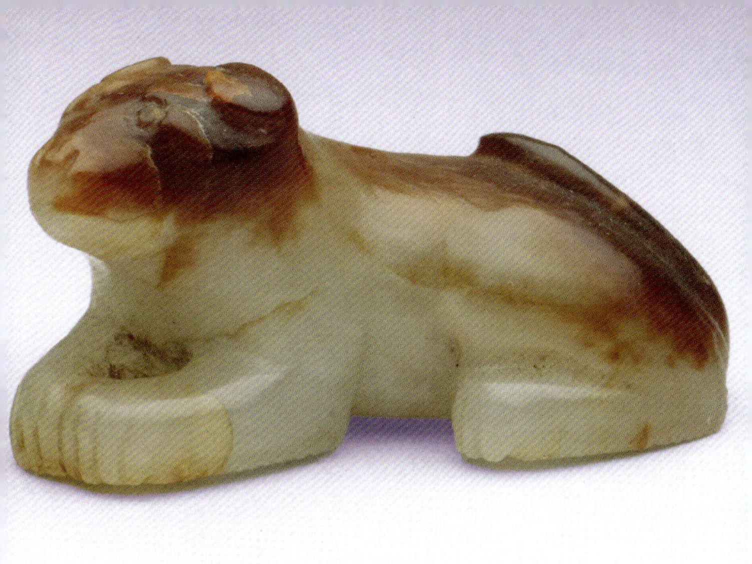

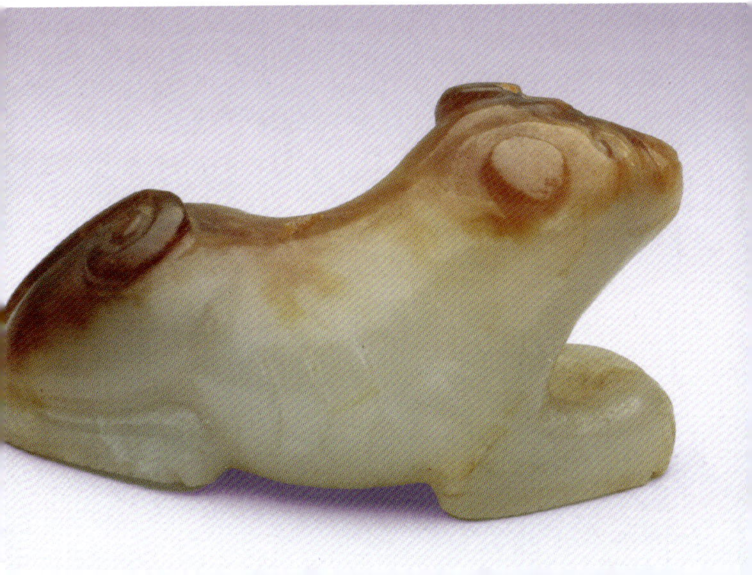

DOG IN FEATHERED HAT AND RUFFLED COLLAR MATCH SAFE

British, late 19th century, silver

Regardless of where you're from, if you were to use this match safe—flip the dog's feet open and grab your match, which has been protected from both the elements and any friction that could cause flames to shoot out of your pocket—you'd need to do so while using a British accent.

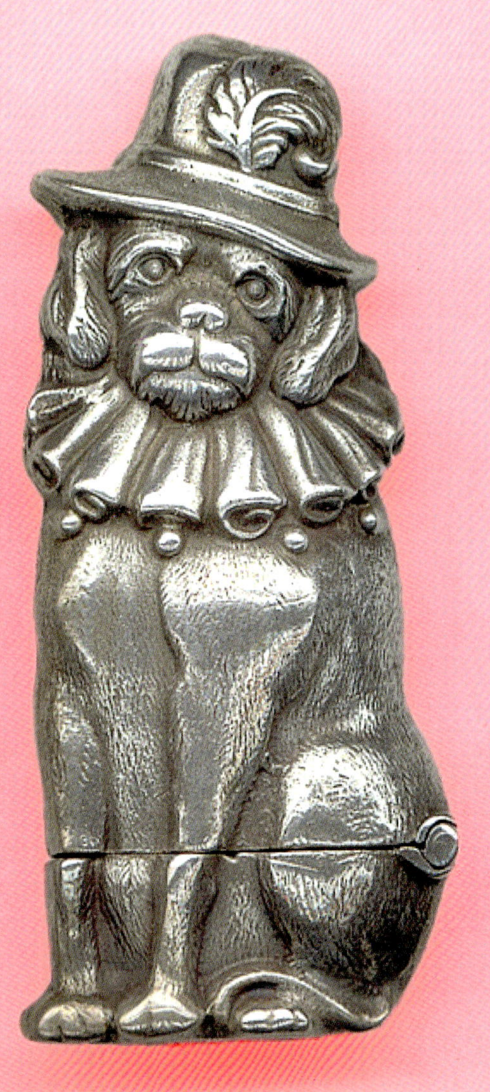

DOG'S HEAD

Eduard Cuypers, Dutch, late 19th century, etching

What we have here is clearly the Einstein of dogs.

This striking etching is by Eduard Cuypers, a Dutch architect whose uncle, Pierre Cuypers (also an architect), designed Amsterdam's Rijksmuseum, which is where this etching lives. Full circle moment![28]

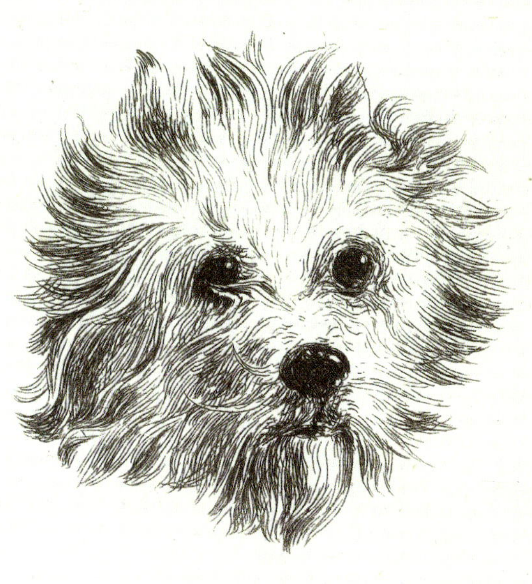

A HOUND AND A BEARDED COLLIE SEATED ON A HUNTING COAT

John Frederick Herring, British, 1855, oil on paper laid on canvas

Have you ever been this cozy?

John Frederick Herring was primarily a painter of hunters on horses. You know the type: red riding coats, horses mid-gallop, the rolling green hills of the English countryside, etc. Beautifully rendered, sure, but not all that interesting to look at.

Occasionally, though, Herring would paint hunting-adjacent scenes, like this pair of pups who found a hunting coat, got cozied up, and had a little snooze. One hundred percent would love to join them.

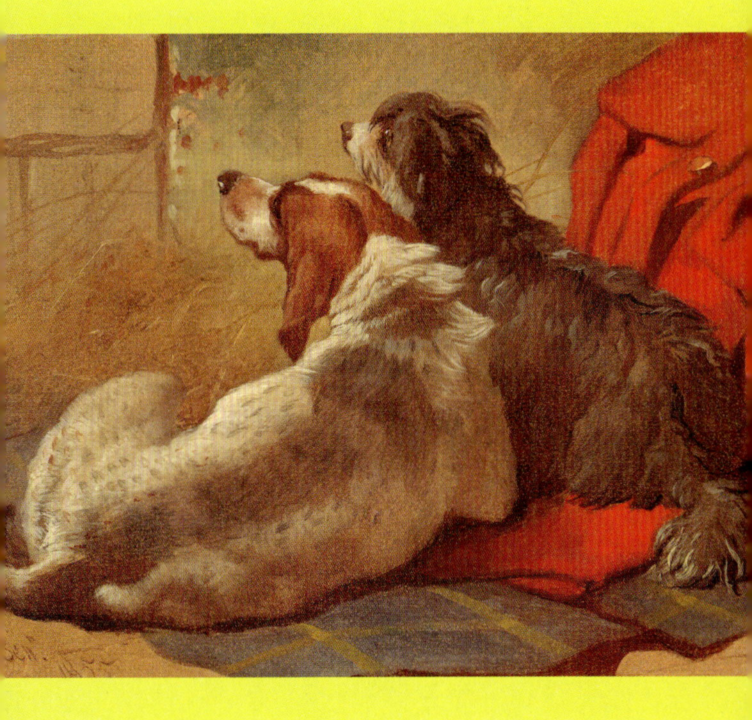

COSMETIC DISH IN THE SHAPE OF A DOG

(front and back views)

Egyptian, 1550–1295 BC, bone

Makers of cosmetic compacts, step up your game. Just look at what they were up to in the New Kingdom era of ancient Egypt! This cosmetics dish—probably for mixing kohl—was made from an incredibly thin piece of bone, exquisitely carved. It's not just cute—it's beautiful. Do you know how much more eye shadow we would buy if it came in containers like this one? Think about it.[29]

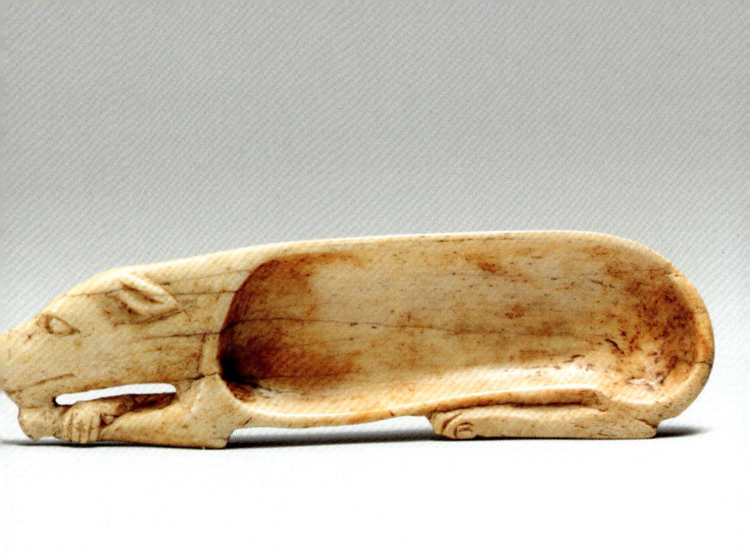

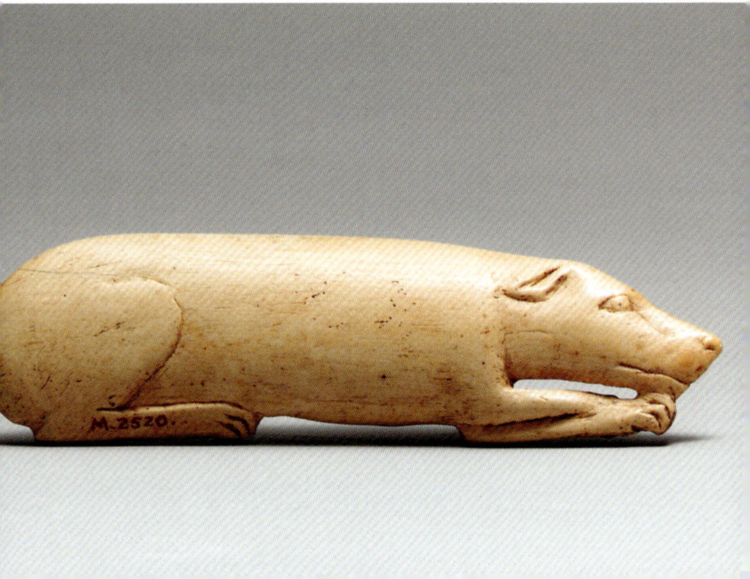

M.2520.

DOG'S HEAD WITH A COLLAR AND RING

Johannes Mock, after Mansfeld, Dutch, 1825, etching

Johannes Mock worked with an unknown artist (noted on the print only as "Mansfeld") to create this extremely endearing etching of a hound dog.

Soon after completing this piece, Mock ditched printing altogether to become a painter. Under the tutelage of Hendrik van de Sande Bakhuyzen, who specialized in painting landscapes featuring cows, Mock began painting—you guessed it—landscapes featuring cows.

Then, having had enough of that, Mock switched subjects completely (who can blame him?) and began painting beaches, boats, and seaside towns, subjects he stuck with for the rest of his life. Way to follow your heart, Johannes. We applaud you.

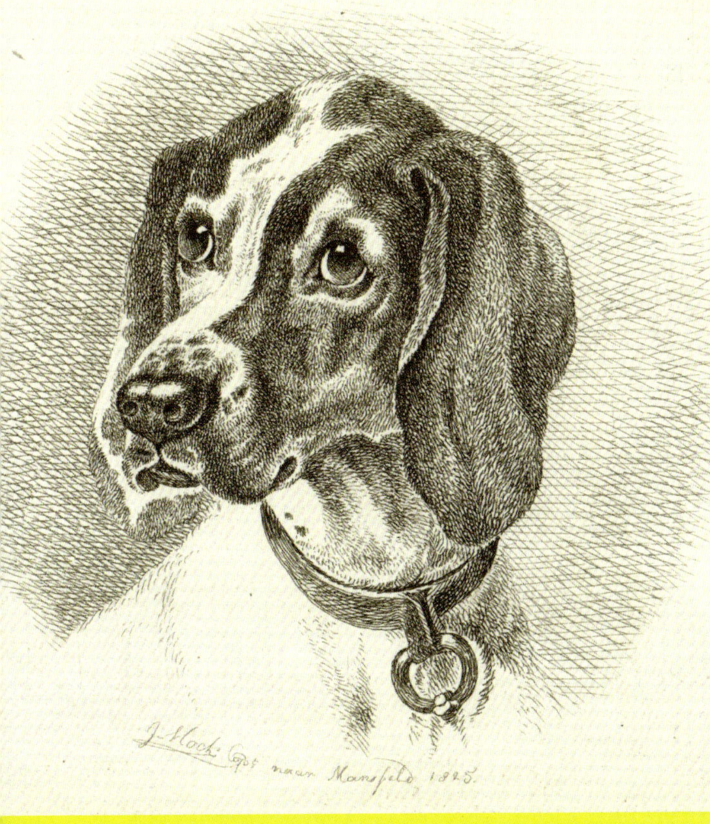
J. Hoch. Copt naar Mansfeld 1825.

MOSAIC IN HOUSE OF LUCIUS CAECILIUS IUCUNDUS

Geremia Discanno, Italian, 1882, chromolithograph from original painting

During the first systematic excavation of Pompeii in 1748, archaeologists were super bummed to find that the frescoes and mosaics that remained (many had already been looted) were not in great shape. They decided they needed to preserve the work by hiring artists to come in and capture them. (Because, you know, photography wasn't invented until 1822.)

Geremia Discanno was one of the artists brought in to do the job. Discanno's paintings were so realistic that more than one expert at the time mistook them for the originals!

This painting is a reproduction of a mosaic from the house of a wealthy banker, Lucius Caecilius Iucundus. If you're ever in Pompeii, you can still see it—and if you do, send me a pic, okay?[30]

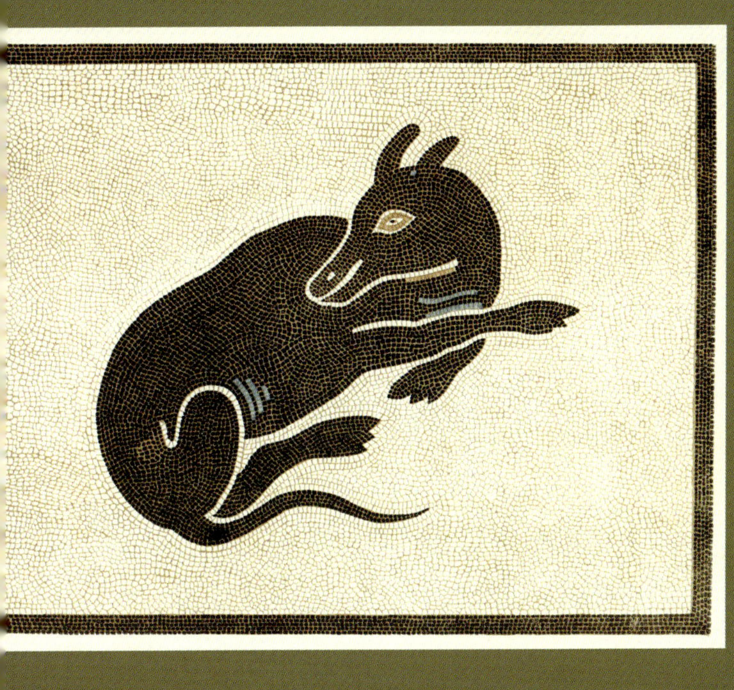

AZOR

Henri-Charles Guérard, French, 1870–1887, etching

Henri-Charles Guérard was the most respected printmaker of his time (the only printer Édouard Manet wanted to work with) and a fantastic artist himself. Ditching sentiment and embracing quirk, Guérard's work is charming as heck.

This is one of many prints he made of his pug Azor, who, despite having a "wouldn't want to meet him in a dark alley" look in this portrait, was, I'm sure, a real sweetheart.

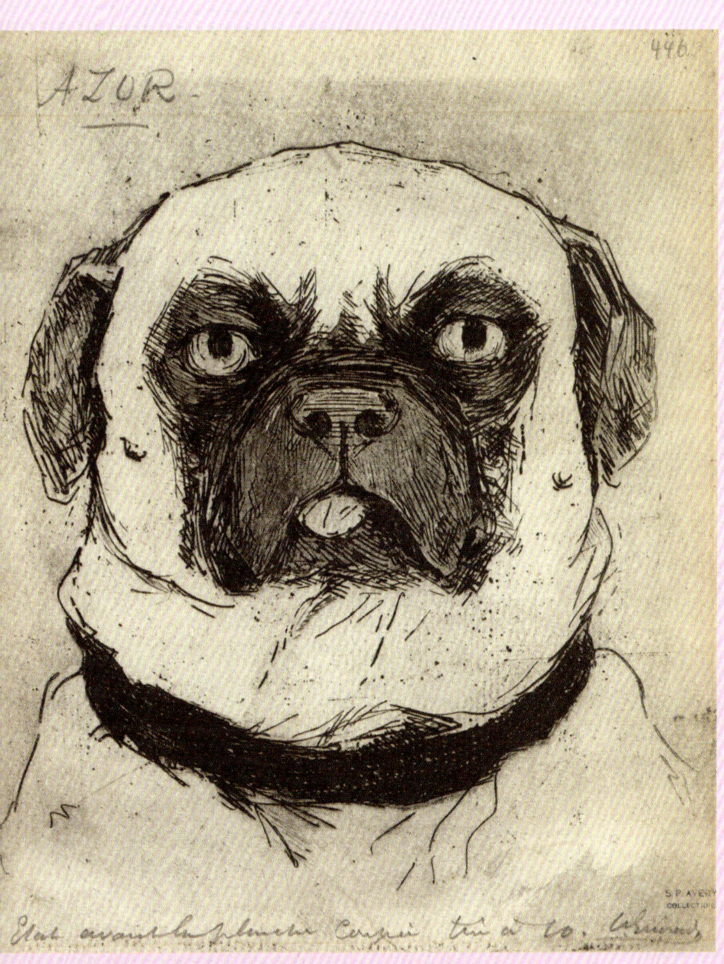
446
AZOR
S.P. AVERY
COLLECTION

HEAD OF A LEONBERGER

Otto Eerelman, Dutch, 1880–1892, paper, chalk, and watercolor on paper

Dutch portrait painter Otto Eerelman was known for his wonderful sitters: He literally taught dogs to sit while he painted them. (Sorry, Mom joke.)

There is a sweetness and tenderness in all of Eerelman's work, and it's coming through loud and clear in this painting of a Leonberger, a breed known for both its size—it reaches an average of 30 inches tall at the shoulder and weighs about 145 pounds—and (luckily) its sweet disposition.

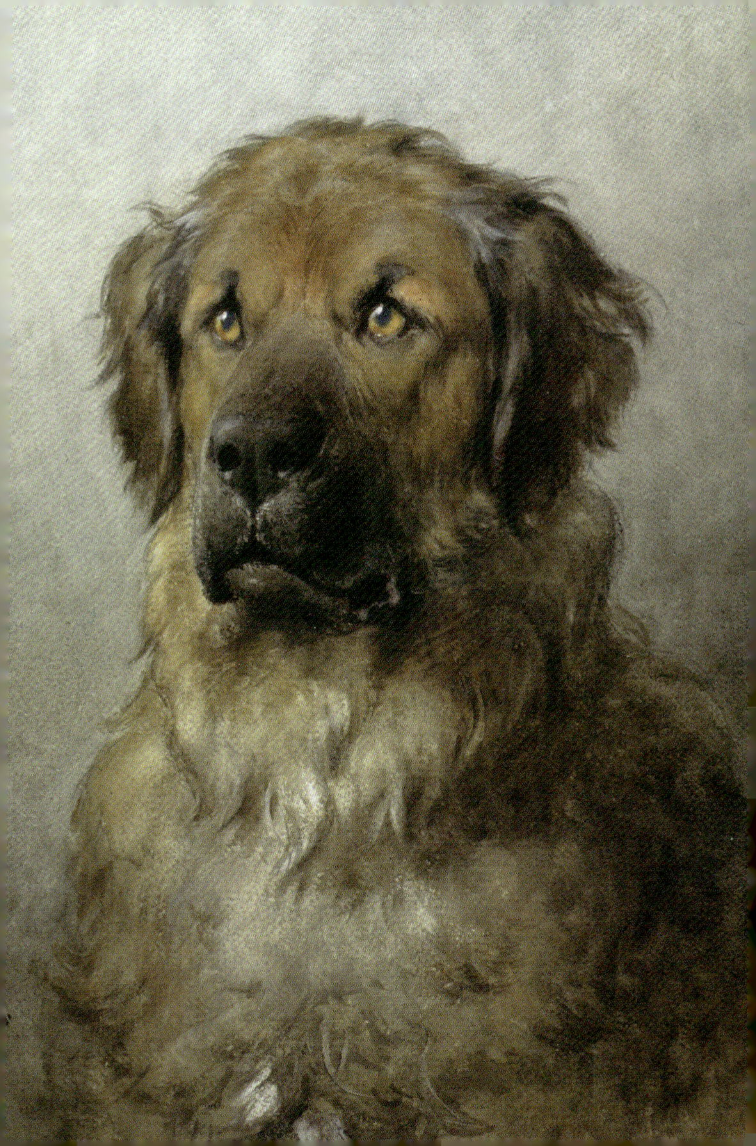

A BLENHEIM SPANIEL

William Webbe, British, ca. 1825, oil on canvas

This is an early work by William Webbe; he would later move toward painting with a level of hyperrealistic—nearly microscopic—detail that was a hallmark of the Pre-Raphaelite movement.

This piece, while still leaning toward realism, also has a lovely soft-focused-ness about it, making it feel like maybe—just maybe—you could walk up and give this frisky li'l friend a hug.[31]

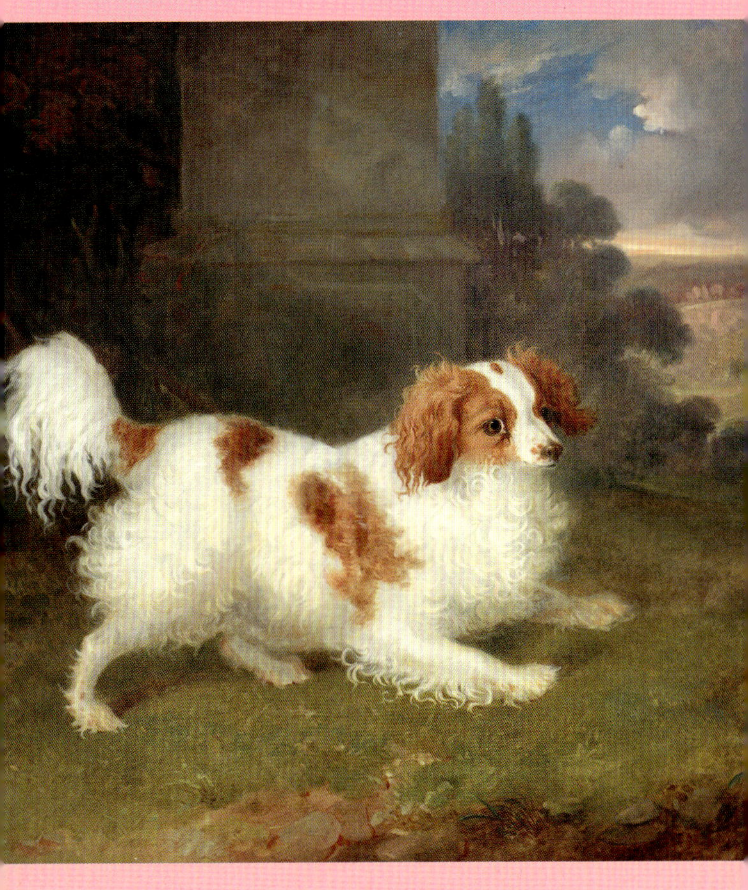

STATUETTE OF A DOG

Roman, 2nd–3rd century, bronze

Ancient Romans absolutely loved their pets, and dogs especially. I think you can tell this sculpture was fashioned after someone's beloved companion. As a remembrance strategy, I find it far less creepy than taxidermy.

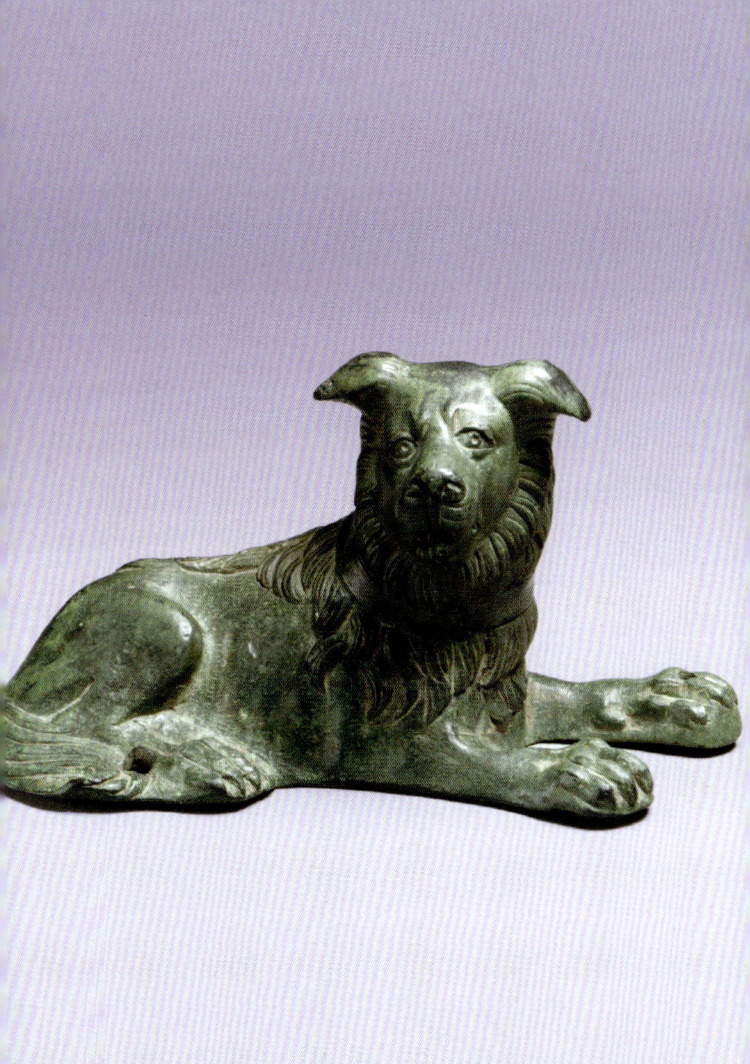

POSTCARD FROM THE WIENER WERKSTÄTTE NO. 677: GREYHOUND

Moriz Jung, Austrian, 1912, color lithograph, Wiener Werkstätte (publisher)

Moriz Jung was a member of the Wiener Werkstätte (Vienna Workshop), an association of fine artists and craftspeople founded in 1903. Inspired by the Arts and Crafts movement in England, the workshop aimed to counteract the effects of industrialization on society by reinvigorating the practice, value, and production of handcrafted artwork—from jewelry and furniture to prints and interior design.

Jung specialized in woodcuts that ranged from the elegant, like this charming greyhound, to the satirical. One such print features two men standing in a cobblestone alley: One plays the violin while the other howls along. The title of that print: *Naturally Gifted Singer*. Burn![32]

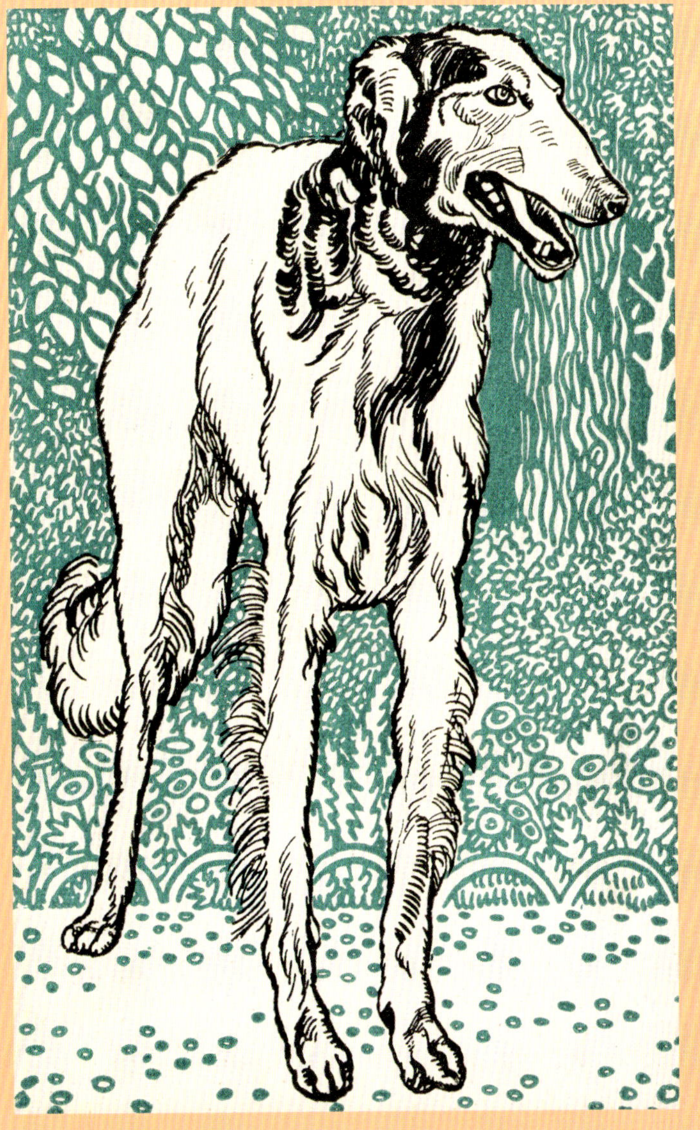

THE LION-DOG OF MALTA—THE LAST OF HIS TRIBE

After Edwin Landseer (artist) and Thomas Landseer (engraver), British, 1844, print

This scene is a bit wacky: Quiz the Maltese is bopping the (unidentified and nonplussed) Saint Bernard on the nose while a mouse munches on a hunk of bread, which the artist had been using as an eraser.

It's even weirder when you find out that the print is based on a painting commissioned by Queen Victoria for her mother. (Quiz was her mother's dog.)

Dogs really do bring out the best in everybody.[33]

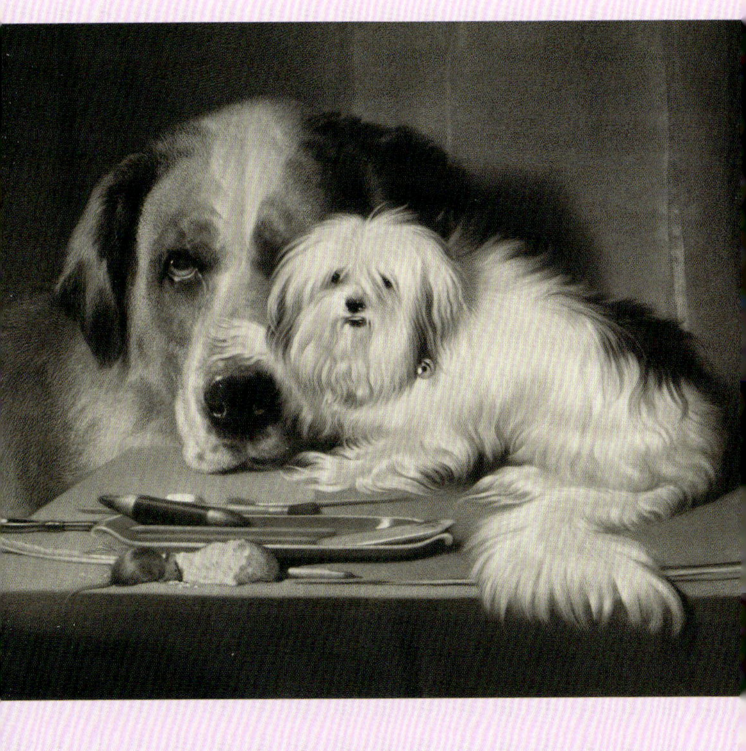

SLEEPING DOG

Rembrandt van Rijn, Dutch, ca. 1640, etching

While dogs occasionally make appearances in Rembrandt's work, this is the only piece we know of with a dog in the starring role. Rembrandt made

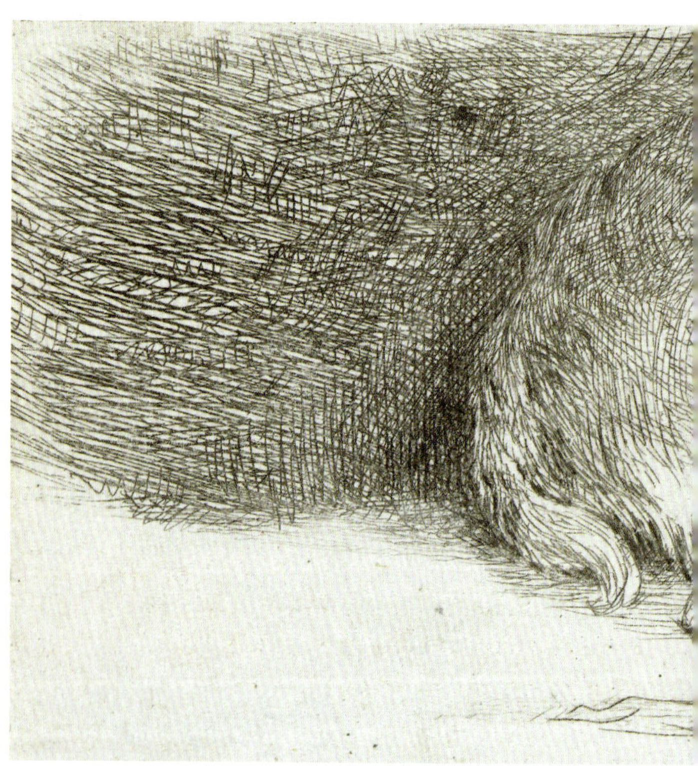

multiple prints from this plate, not only making adjustments to the plate itself to achieve the results he wanted, but also cropping the image after it was printed. This crop enhances the feeling that the puppy is snuggling up into a very cozy spot.[34]

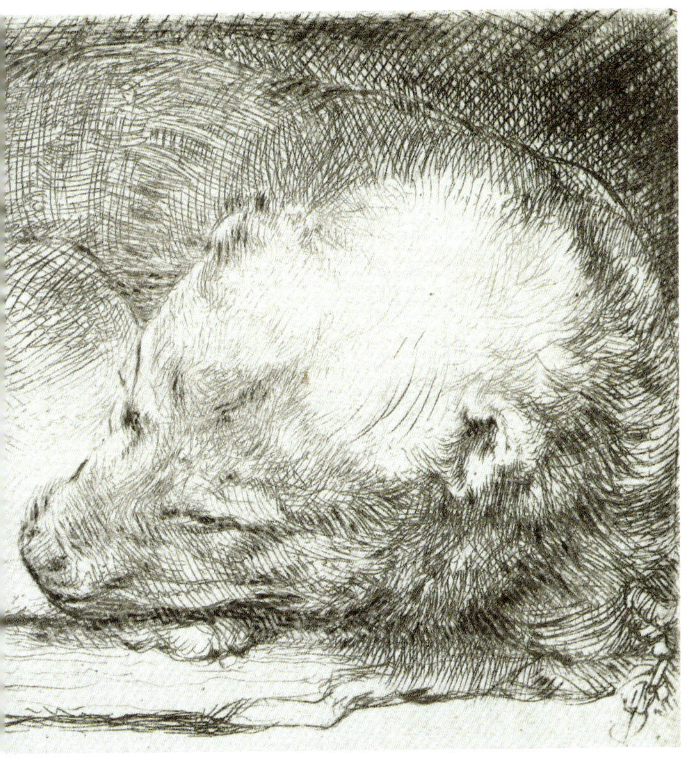

TWO DOGS

Henri de Toulouse-Lautrec, French, 19th century
undated, pen and ink on paper

The artist Henri de Toulouse-Lautrec is mostly known for his sometimes racy, often cynical paintings of Parisian nightlife, making this whimsical little drawing especially sweet.

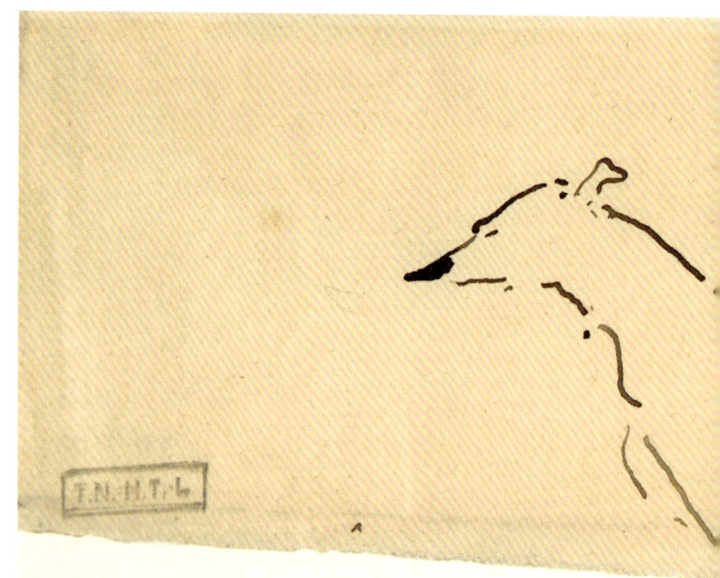

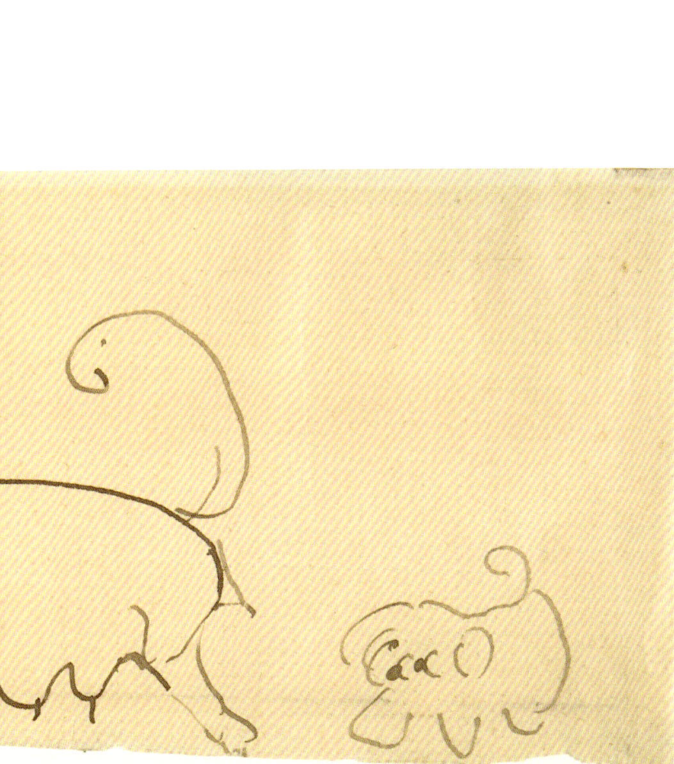

SIX RECLINING HUNTING DOGS

Wenceslaus Hollar, German, 1647, etching

There are literally hundreds of artworks featuring hunting dogs. I've included very few of them here, but this one made the cut because the dog on the bottom right licking its rather prominent . . . situation is so hilarious, I couldn't resist.

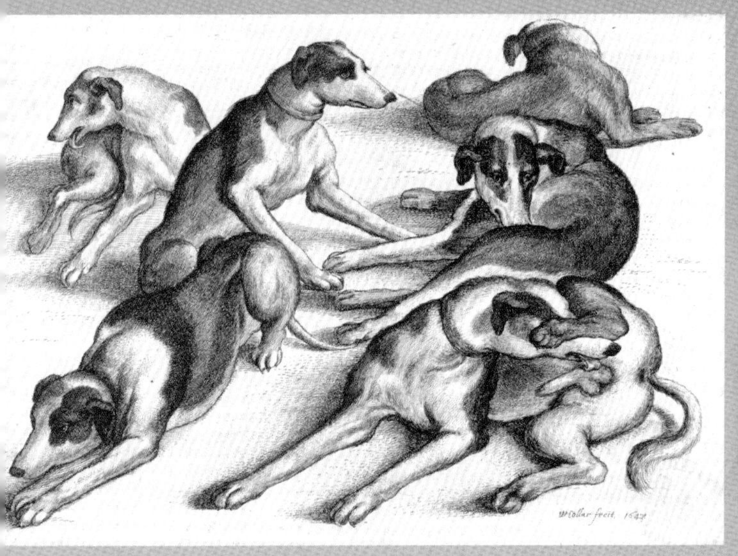
WHollar fecit.

DOOR KNOCKER IN THE SHAPE OF A SMALL DOG

Spanish, 15th–16th century, wrought iron

During the Middle Ages, Spanish ironsmiths cranked out all kinds of practical objects, such as armor and nails. But some liked to mix it up a bit: This doggie door knocker (and its curlicue tail!) is one example. Way to add whimsy, anonymous Spanish ironsmith—we love it!

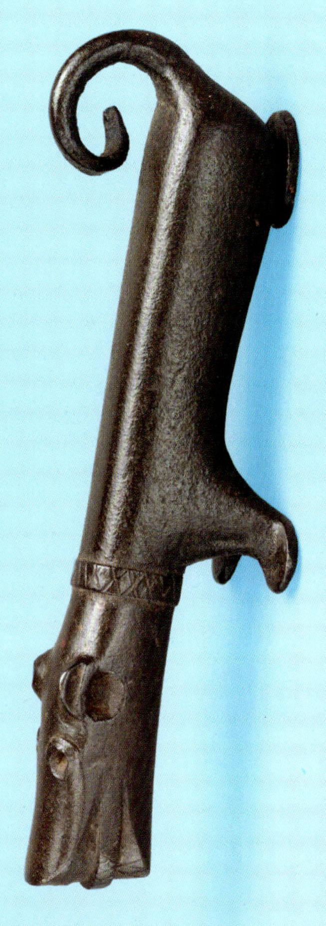

HUNTING DOG

European, 15th–16th century, wrought iron

Wrought iron pieces are created by heating iron, then pounding it with the flat side of an anvil. The other side, a pointed cone, is used to create curves. Given some of the details on this piece, like the collar, the artist may have also used cold iron techniques, chiseling some of the finer details.

Whatever techniques were used, let's just take a minute to appreciate an artisan who created a silhouette this delicate, balanced, and graceful out of a shapeless lump of lava-hot iron.[35]

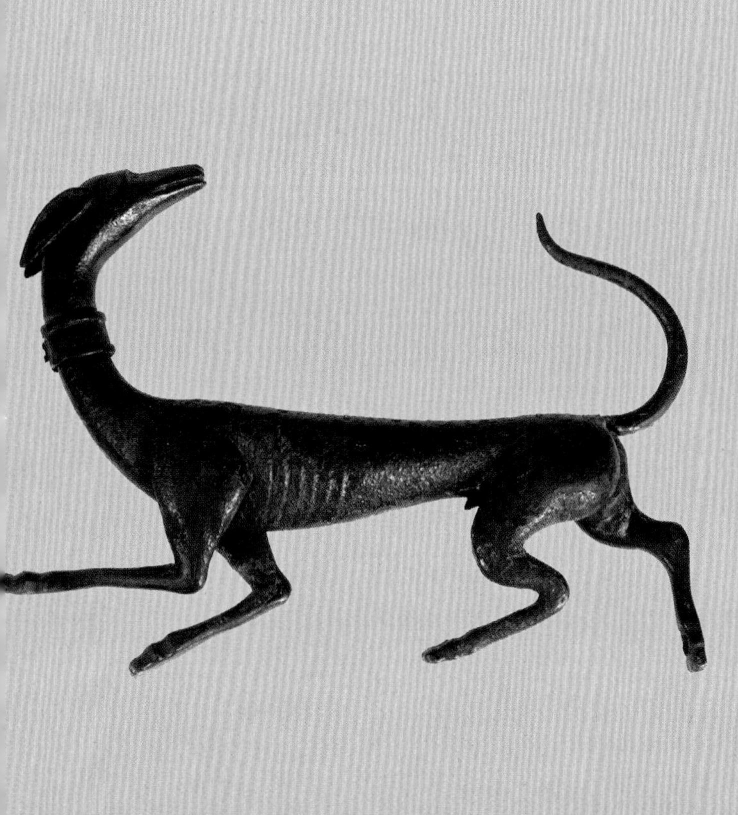

TWO STUDIES OF A POODLE

Gustav Klimt, Austrian, 1902–1904, pencil on packing paper

Creator of many ethereal maximalist paintings—most famously *The Kiss*—Gustav Klimt offers in this sketch a lovely minimalist moment.

Apparently Klimt was more into cats than dogs: One visitor spotted at least eight of them making mayhem in his studio (dogs would never).

Perhaps one of his (many, many, many) lady friends or models brought poodles to his studio? Poodles didn't appear in any of Klimt's other work, so we'll just have to make do with imagining what they might have looked like in his signature style, nestled among a riot of fabrics and flowers.[36]

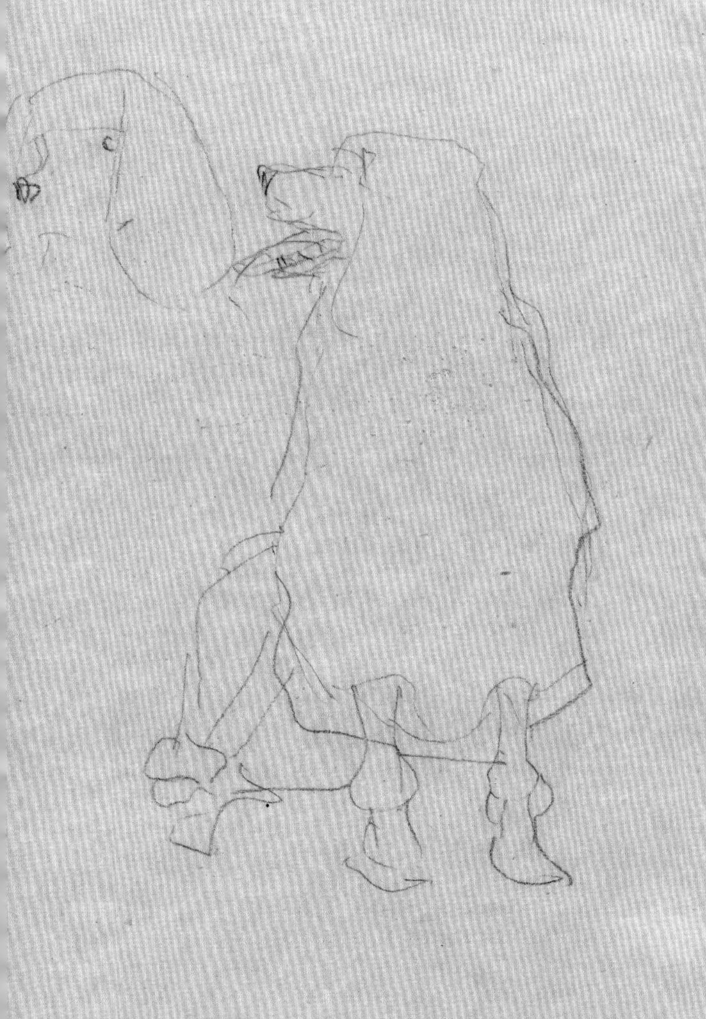

AMULET OF A DOG

Egyptian, 2123–2040 BC,
turquoise-green faience

Amulets were everywhere in ancient Egypt, worn or carried by almost everyone. This one uses a material called faience, inexpensively made from a mix of sand, quartz pebbles, and limestone, then fired until it shone like its more expensive look-alike, turquoise. Some amulets were worn for protection, but others may have simply been a reminder of a favorite pet. Awwwww.

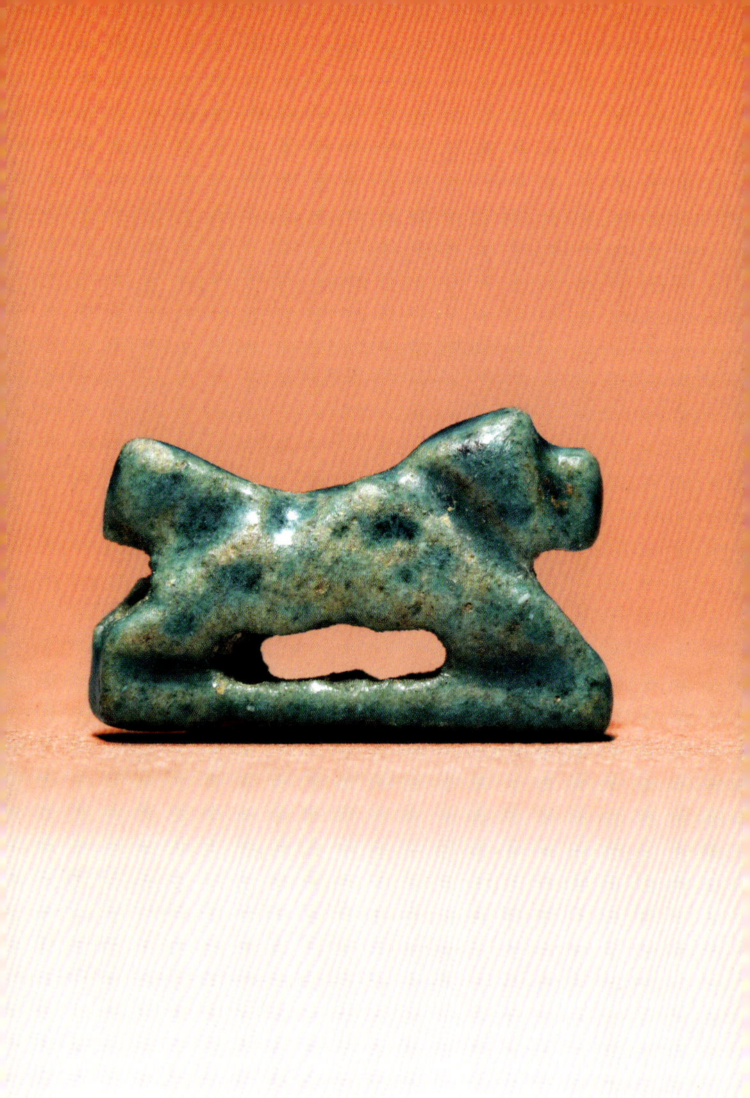

INCENSE BOXES IN THE SHAPE OF DOG CHARMS

Japanese, 1840, porcelain with overglaze enamels

Dogs like these, which always came in pairs, were traditional Japanese wedding gifts, symbolizing luck and bringing protection to the couple and their future children. In the later part of the Edo period, they were also incorporated into the wedding ceremony itself, carried with the bride on a palanquin (or *norimono* in Japanese—a covered chair used to transport the bride to her groom). As wedding gifts go, I'd take these over a fondue set any day, amiright?

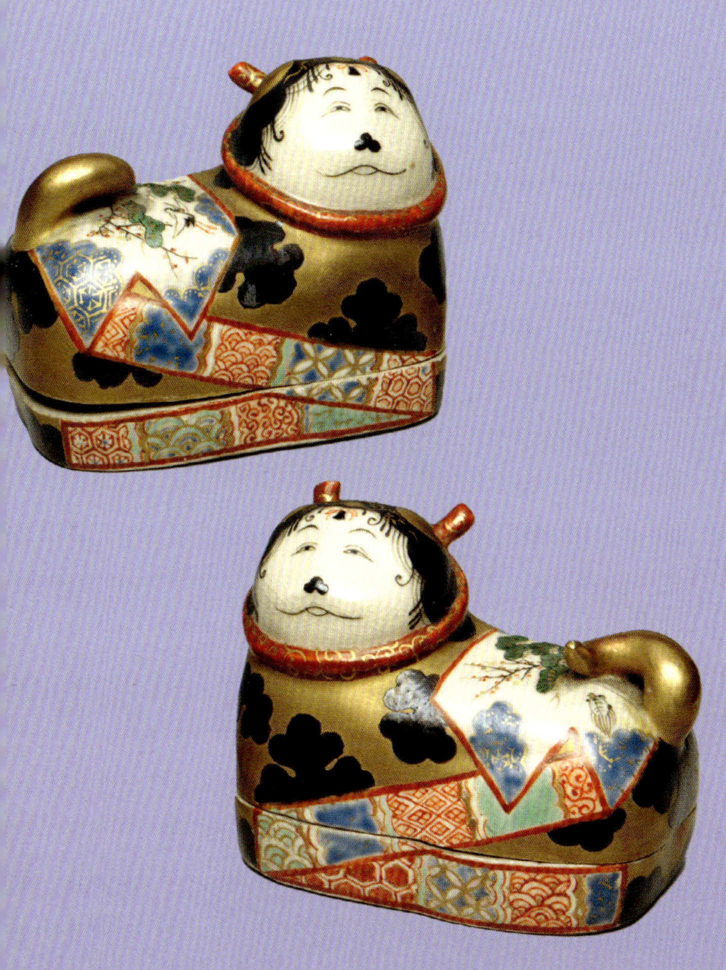

HOUND

Italian, 19th–20th century, porcelain

"Get that tail! Get it! You get that tail ya little rascal—before it gets you!"

Is this inscribed somewhere on the statue? No. But it could be.

We don't know anything about the sculptor of this piece, but we do know that they really understood what dogs like to get up to.

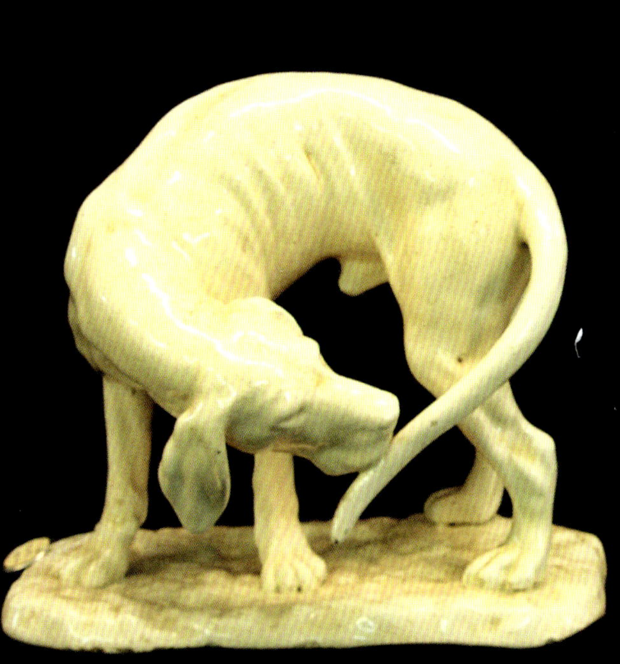

STICK PIN WITH HOUND'S HEAD

British, 1870s, gold, lapis lazuli, and enamel

Stick pins were popular with men in the nineteenth century, worn in either a tie or—if you were especially posh—a cravat.

But to avoid any whiff of femininity (eye roll), the pins were primarily shaped like animals or objects related to manly pursuits, like hunting and sports (another eye roll). Think horses, foxes, fish, skulls and crossbones, etc.

But pins could also signify deeper meanings, including indicating that the person was in mourning, making it possible to wear your heart on your cravat, if you will.

Whatever the meaning, if I saw anyone wearing this hound's head pin, I'd definitely introduce myself and, eventually, try to get them to give it to me.

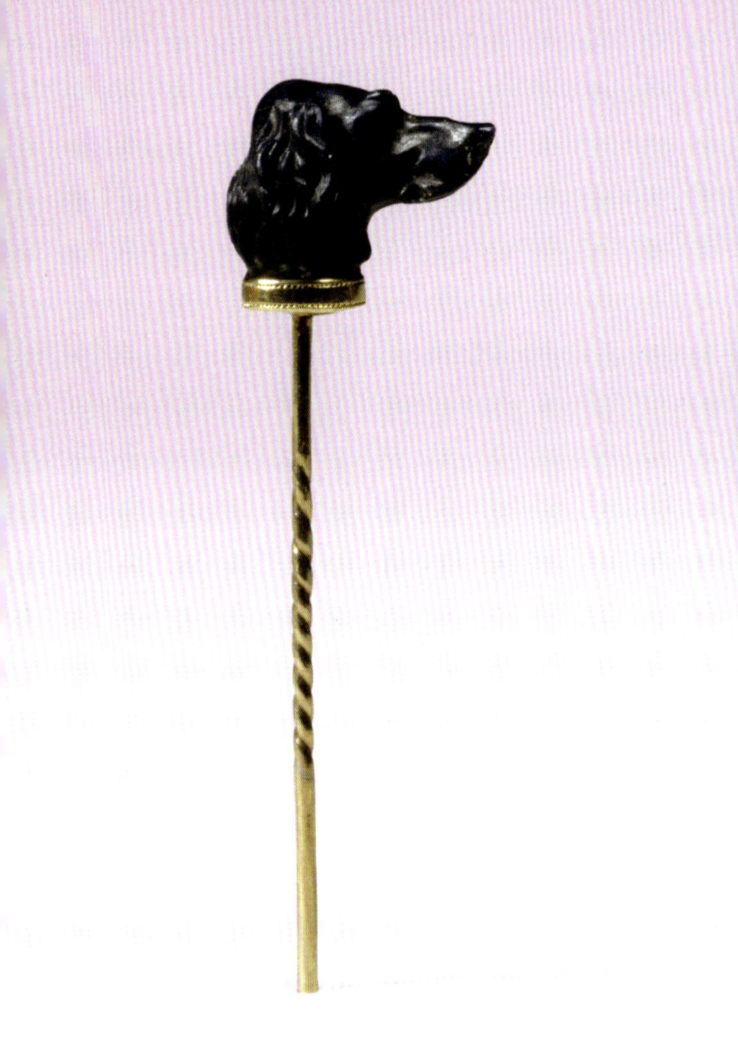

ONE OF TEN NOBLE DOGS, NAMED MO-YU CH'IH

Giuseppe Castiglione, Chinese (Qing Dynasty), 1700s, painting, color on silk

You may have noticed that Giuseppe Castiglione is not a Chinese name, and that is because he was not, in fact, Chinese.

Castiglione was an Italian Jesuit monk who was sent as a missionary to Beijing. His talents for drawing and painting put him on the radar of the Chinese emperor, who wanted to commission artwork that a) pumped up the ol' ego, and b) showed off all his special royal stuff.

This portrait of a Chinese greyhound named Mo-yu Ch'ih is one in a series Castiglione completed of the emperor's ten favorite dogs—a series titled, depending on the translation, "Ten Noble Dogs" or "Ten Prized Dogs." I feel bad for all of the nonnoble/nonprized dogs that were not included.[37]

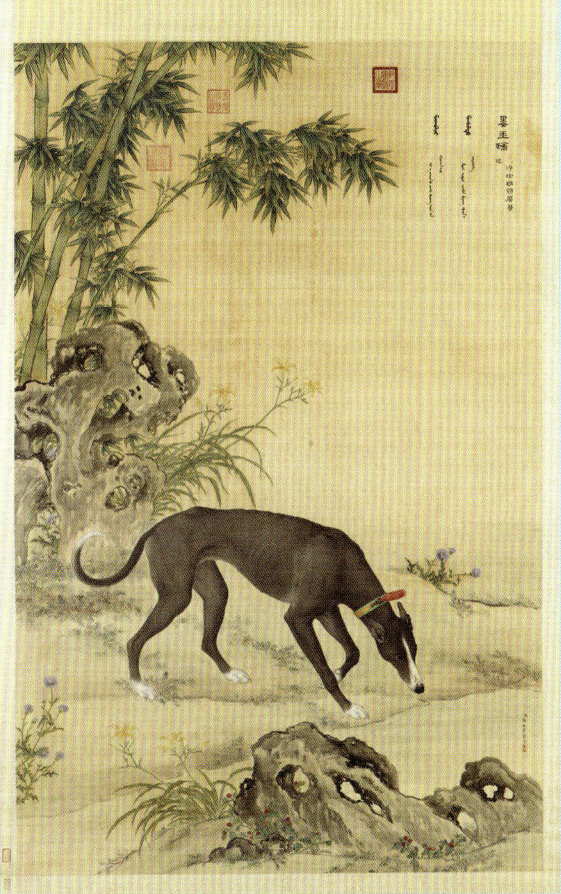
墨玉螭

DOG

Julie de Graag, Dutch, 1917, woodcut

Julie de Graag specialized in woodcuts, preferring to use the end grain of the wood—even though it was more difficult to carve—because it produced a sharper, more defined image when printed.

Whether images of people, plants, animals, or landscapes, de Graag's bold work edges toward abstraction and has a stately, almost reverent vibe. So good.

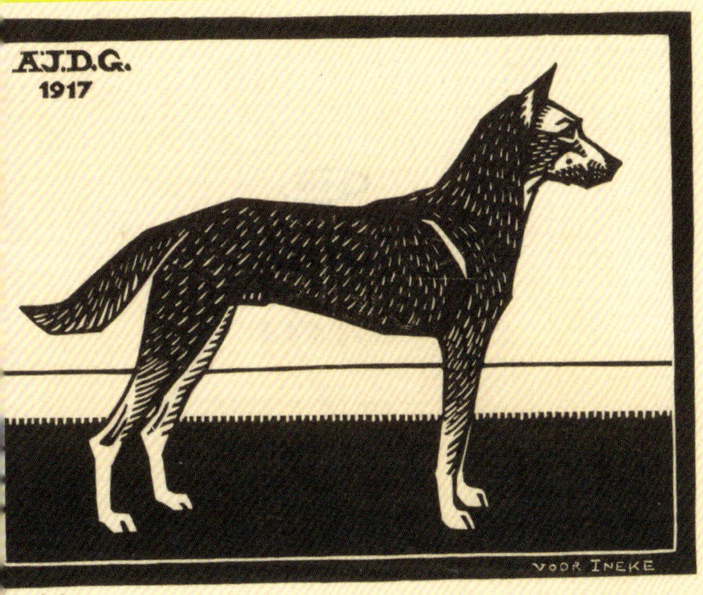
A.J.D.G.
1917
VOOR INEKE

DOG STUDY *and* TWO SEATED BASSET HOUNDS

Emmanuel Frémiet, French, ca. 1850 and 1853, graphite drawing on paper; bronze

This is a fun one—we get to see both a sculpture and a sketch that part of the sculpture was based on.

These basset hound puppies, Ravageot and Ravageole, belonged to Napoléon III (no, not that Napoléon, his nephew), who ruled France from 1850 to 1870.

At first it seems like the dog on the left, Ravageole, is looking dejected, but no! Look carefully and you'll see that she's watching the movements of a very tiny—and presumably very slow—snail on the ground in front of her. Good one, Mr. Frémiet.[38]

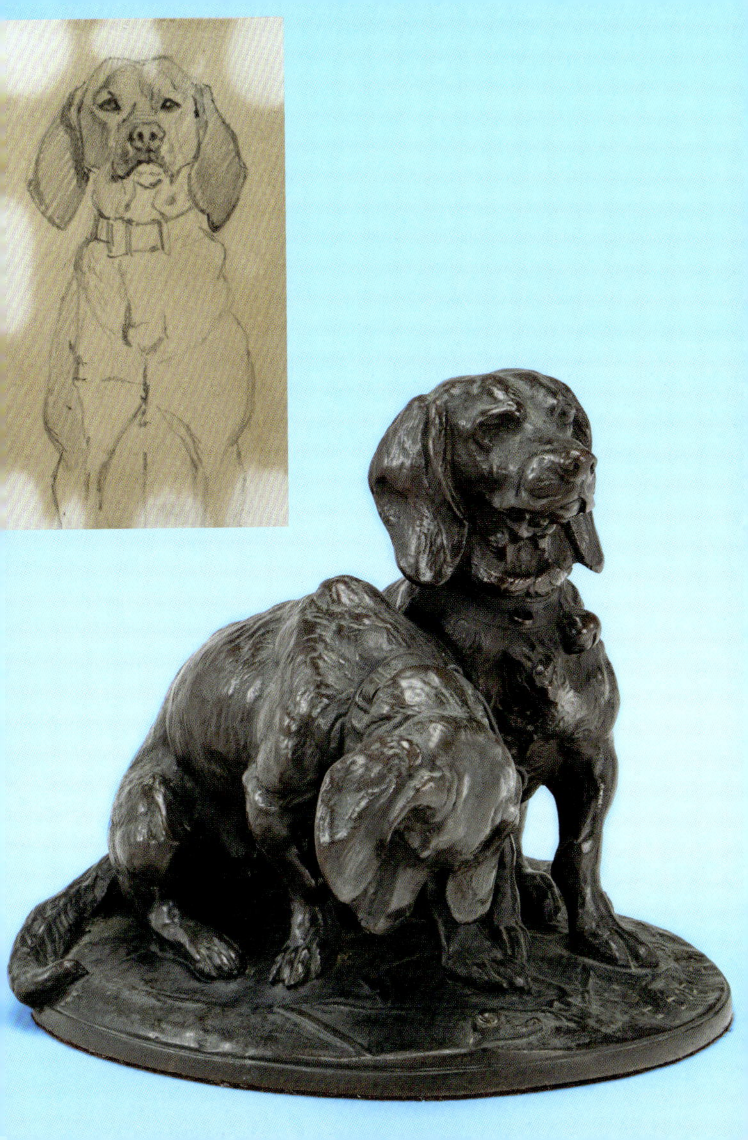

POINTER DOG HEAD

Nicolas-Toussaint Charlet, French, 1828, print on paper

Artist Nicolas-Toussaint Charlet was primarily known for his rendering of military figures and battle scenes. When that's your main gig, sometimes you need a break. I'm glad he took time out to make this sweet picture of a pointer.

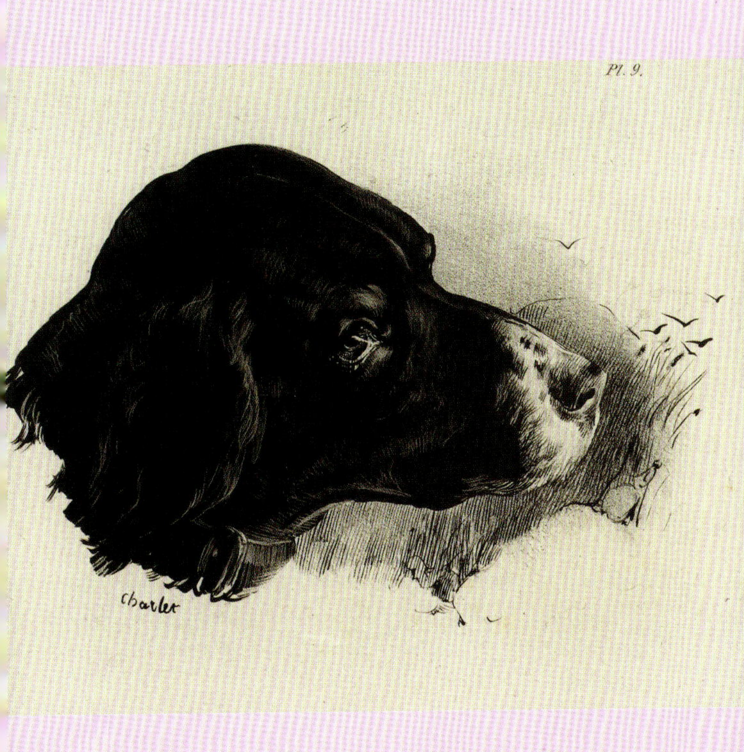

Pl. 9.

BUTTON, PAINTED WITH A DOG

French, undated, porcelain

This hand-painted button of a little brown and white hound doesn't have a date on it, but in eighteenth-century Paris, painted porcelain buttons were all the rage.

Dogs, flowers, boats, people: Painted buttons could depict absolutely anything of interest to the wearer, including something a bit . . . spicy. Buttons with scandalous subject matter could be sewn behind a lapel, where they could be shared as opportunities presented themselves.

Ostentatious buttons were already a thing in France before this trend: Louis XIV's favorite coat reportedly had a whopping 123 buttons, each one blinged out with diamonds. He probably wore it over his bejeweled suit, which is said to have had so many gems he could barely move in it.[39]

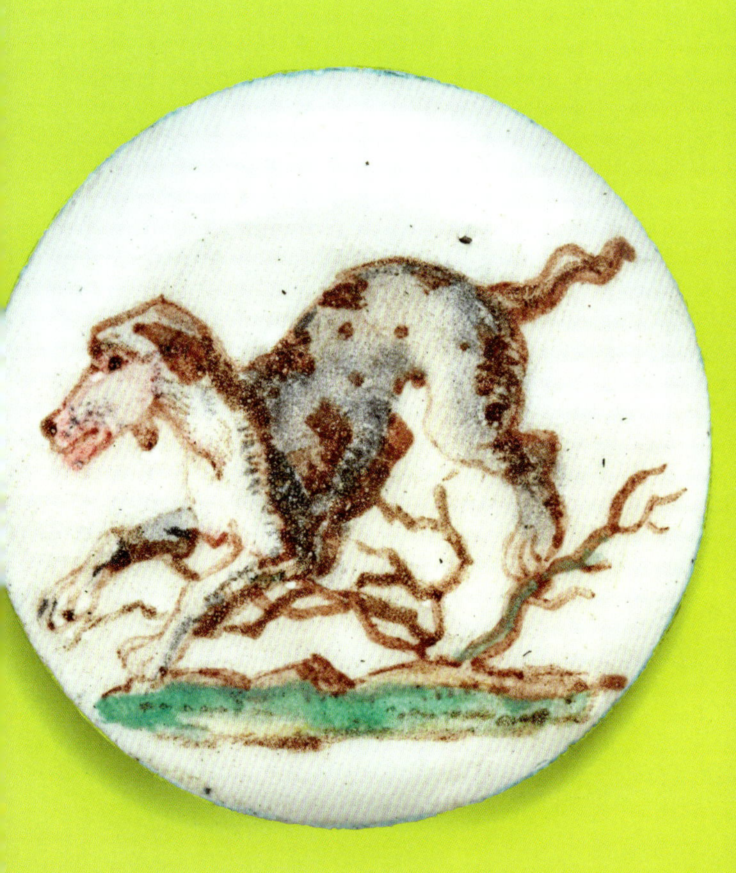

STATUETTE OF MUNITO THE POODLE

Jean-Pierre Dantan, French, 1840, bronze

Munito was a performing poodle who was quite a star in his day. During his shows, his manager, Signor Castelli, would ask Munito math and science questions, and—by indicating a card on the ground in front of him—Munito would unfailingly choose the correct answer.

Munito's fans included the prince regent, the Duke of York, and Charles Dickens, who believed he had spotted the trick. After catching a whiff of aniseed as Castelli walked by, Dickens theorized that Munito was being tipped off to the correct answers by scent.

A more likely explanation, however, was that Castelli was breaking a toothpick hidden in his pocket when the dog was in front of the right card—a sound that only Munito would hear.

Whether it was his extraordinary sense of smell or hearing that was the key to Munito's success, I think we can all agree that he was extraordinary indeed.[40]

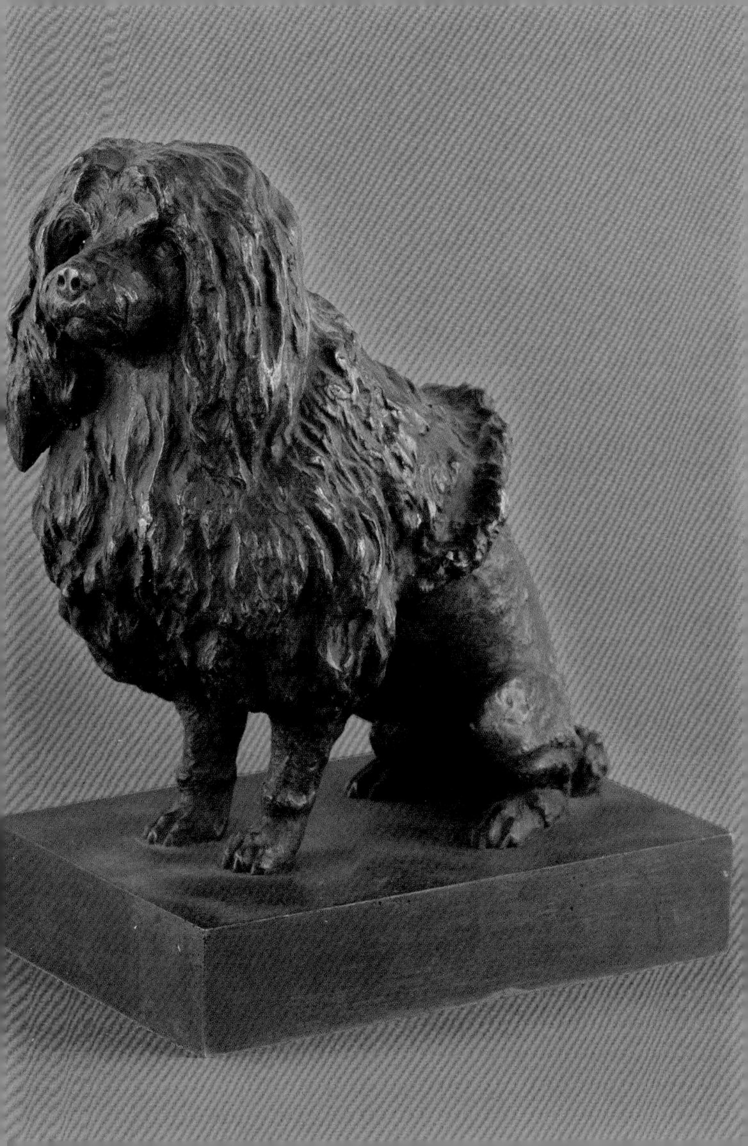

DOG HEAD STIRRUP CUP

British, 1810–1820, ceramic

If you, like me, thought a stirrup cup was some fancy thing you put your foot into while riding a horse, then, like me, you would be wrong.

Turns out a stirrup cup is handed to a guest who's ready to skedaddle, already on their horse with their feet in the stirrups, a little sip of something boozy before they go.

"Ah, before you take your leave, have a stirrup cup, my good mate!" you say. Perched atop their trusty steed, your friend gulps down their port, hands the cup back, tips their hat, and gallops off into the sunset, the memory of your generous hospitality lingering in their mouth and heart.[41]

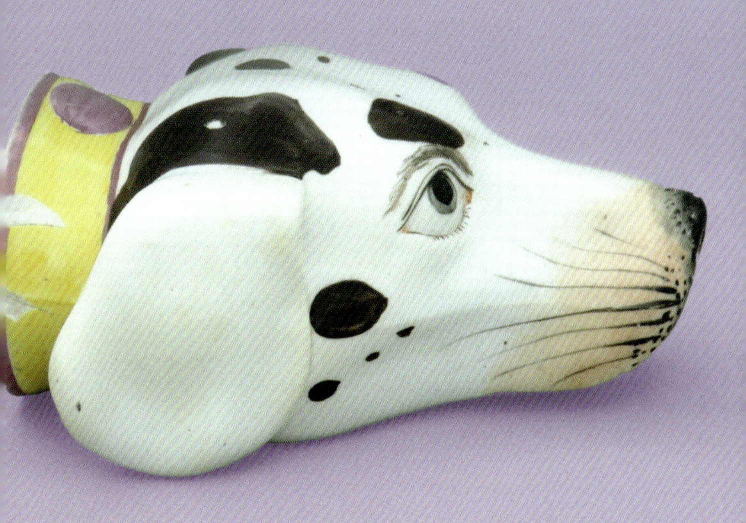

A TALE OF TWO TAMAS

In 1873, French banker and art collector Henri Cernuschi went to Japan and brought back a Japanese spaniel named Tama ("jewel" in Japanese). Cernuschi and a friend each commissioned a portrait of Tama: one from Pierre-Auguste Renoir and one from Édouard Manet. (Nice friends to have around, right?)[42]

TAMA, THE JAPANESE DOG

Pierre-Auguste Renoir, French, ca. 1876, oil on canvas

Renoir's painting may be a winking reference to portraits made of the horses of kings, like those Anthony van Dyck made for Charles I. Tallyho, Tama!

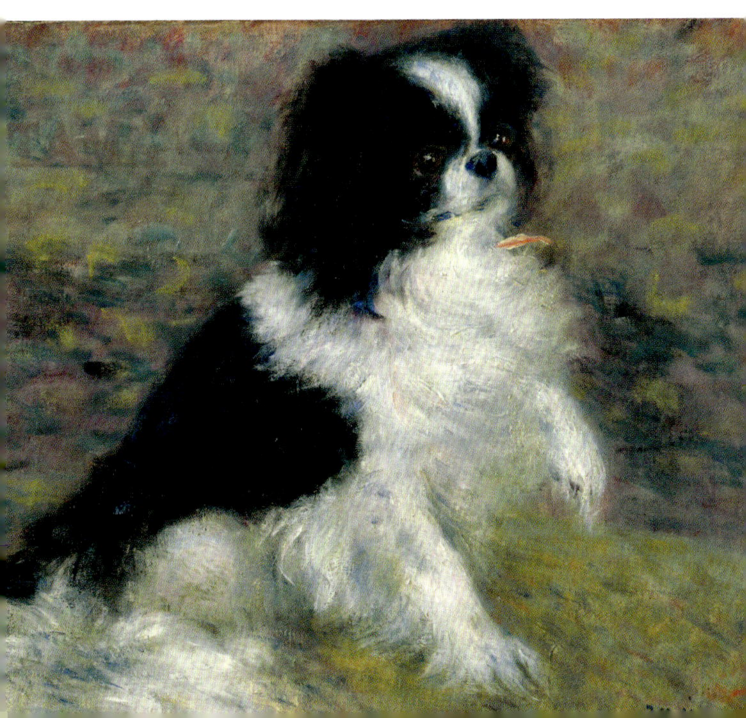

TAMA, THE JAPANESE DOG

Édouard Manet, French, ca. 1875, oil on canvas

Manet's portrait is a bit feistier, with Tama having just defeated a nemesis: a Japanese doll.

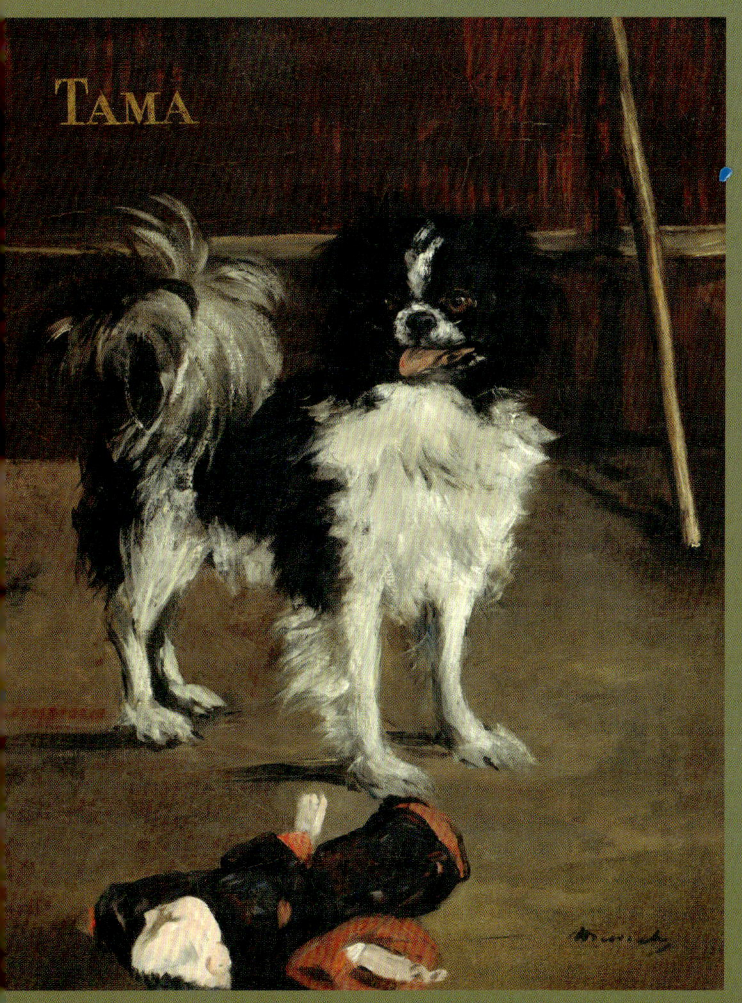
TAMA

PUPPY WITH A SLICE OF DRIED SALMON

Totoya Hokkei, Japanese, 1825, woodblock print

In Japan, one New Year's tradition is creating a *kadomatsu*, an arrangement of young pine sprigs and bamboo. The *kadomatsu* was placed in front of your house as an offering to your ancestors in exchange for their blessing on your year.

A poem on this woodblock print, created in celebration of New Year's 1825, reads, in part, "People go out to pull young pine . . . [and] even a puppy in the field has learned to pull things."

So it's basically an 1825-style meme: We're out here snagging pine sprigs for our *kadomatsu*; this rascal's out here snagging dried salmon. Charming as heck.

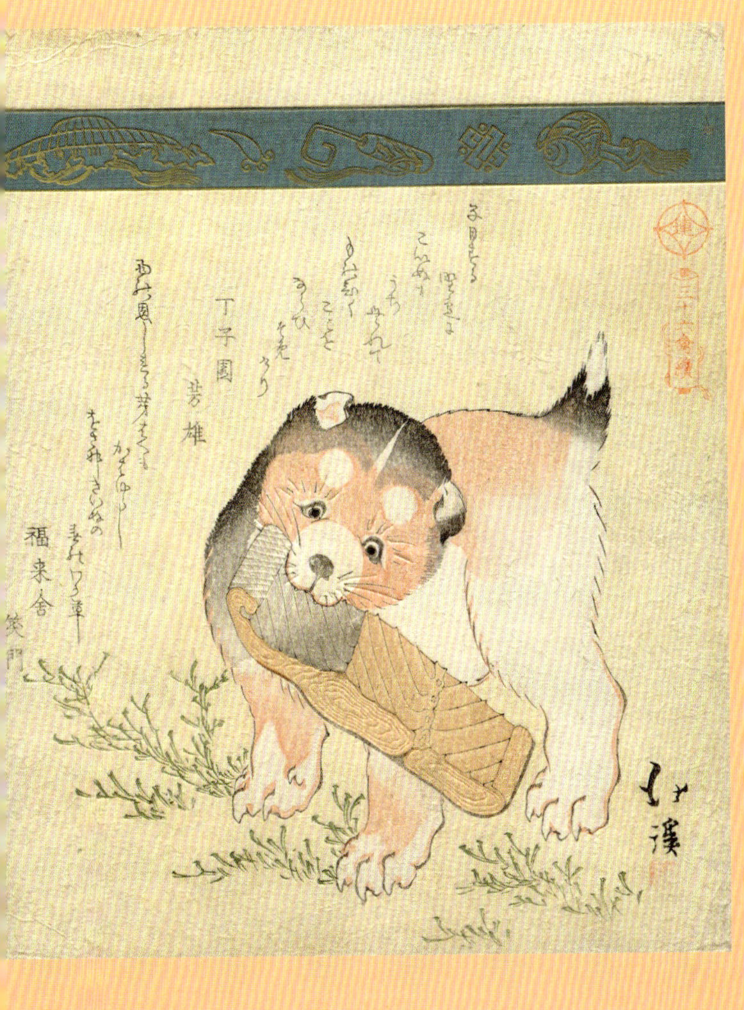

丁子園
芳雄
福来舎

HEAD OF A DOG

Pierre-Auguste Renoir, French, 1870, oil on canvas

Renoir painted this dog in 1870, right around the time that several paintings he had submitted for exhibition at the salon of the Académie des Beaux-Arts were rejected.

It was the last straw for Renoir: He was fed up with the Académie's ultraclassical aesthetic and their stranglehold on public taste. They were also gatekeeping artistic opportunities: Getting your work accepted into one of their exhibitions was basically like going viral.

By 1874, Renoir and other artists, including Edgar Degas, Camille Pissarro, and Mary Cassatt, had started their own artistic society (eventually becoming known as Impressionists), complete with their own salons.

And thank heavens they did: I'm pretty sure the world did not need any more paintings with titles like *The Death of Socrates* or *The Dead Christ with Angels*. Here, Renoir has captured the warm essence of this little pup using loose brushstrokes, reflected light, and obvious affection. Now that's more like it.[43]

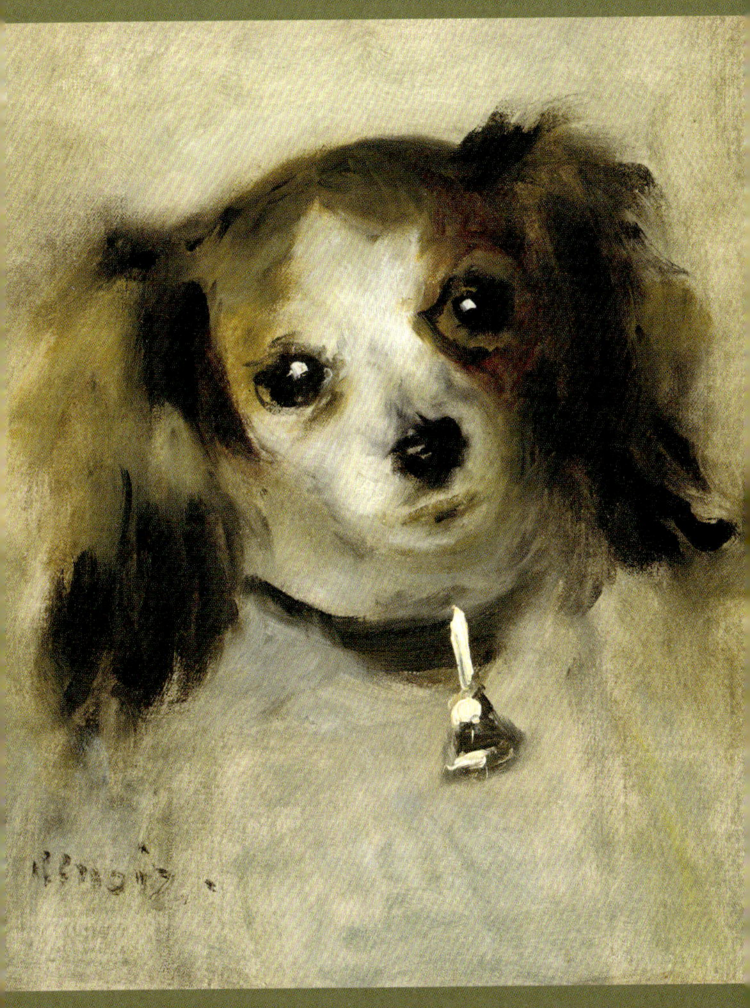

"CANIS MAJOR," ILLUSTRATION IN *URANIA'S MIRROR*

Sidney Hall, British, 1825, print on layered paper board: etching, hand-colored

An illustration of the constellation Canis Major as a greyhound is printed on this card, one of thirty-two that came in a box titled *Urania's Mirror*. (Urania is the muse of astronomy, but you probably already knew that.) See the stars all over his body? Sure, those are the stars in the constellation, but they're also holes! When you lift the card to the light, you see the pattern of the constellation, which you can then look for in the sky! Who needs apps? Absolutely brilliant.[44]

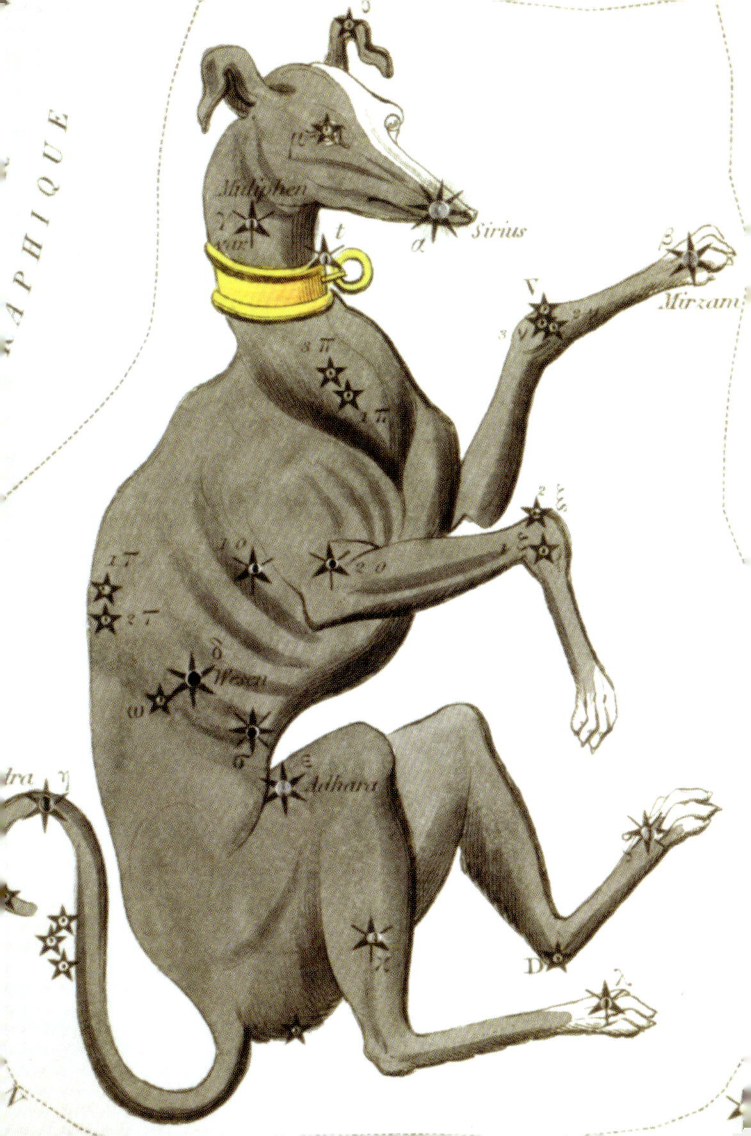
RAPHIQUE
Sirius
Mirzam
Adhara

GOLD-WEIGHT: DOG

West African (Akan), 19th century, brass

From as far back as the 1400s up until the 1890s, the Akan people of West Africa used *mrammuo*, or brass weights, to measure gold dust for sale and trade. In the seventeenth century, artisans decided to spice things up, changing *mrammuo* forms from geometric designs to figurative shapes such as plants, animals, people, and objects. The figures held many layers of meaning related to Akan proverbs and culture.

One possible association for this little brass babe: Of the seven Akan clans, one, Aduana, has the dog as its totem. According to legend, the dog, with a flame in its mouth and gold in its cheeks, lit the way for the clan on its journey to a new land, Dormaa, where the flame still burns. Dog: guide and keeper of the flame. Love it.[45]

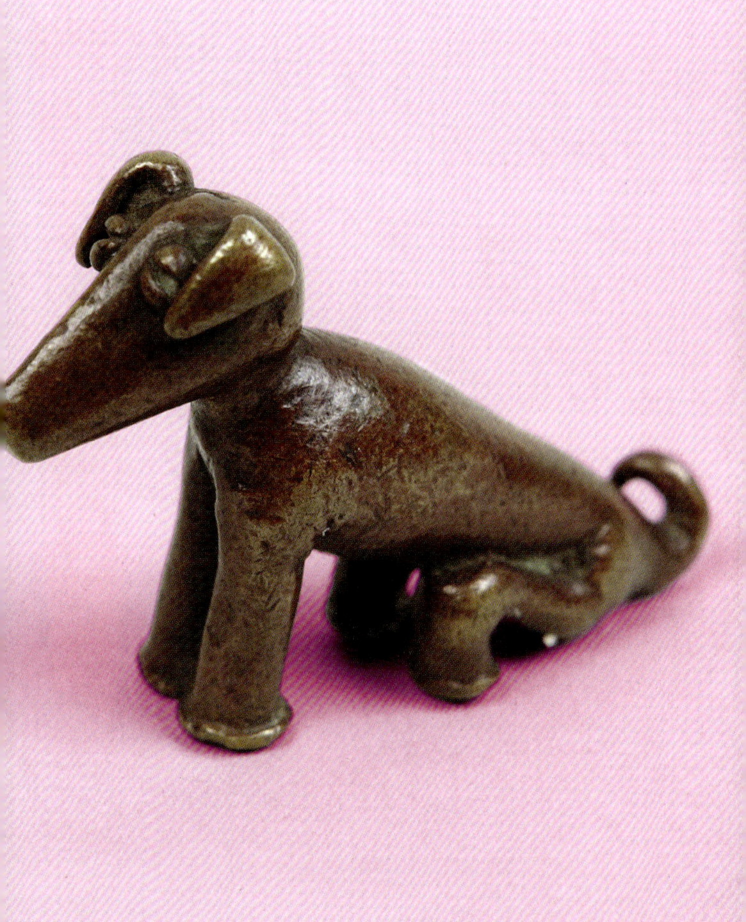

ILLUSTRATION FROM *TRAVELS OF SIR JOHN MANDEVILLE*

German, 1459, drawings on paper

Sir John Mandeville may have been a real person, but he was definitely *not* the author of *Travels of Sir John Mandeville*, as the book itself claims. In fact, there is speculation that whoever wrote it probably never traveled at all, since most of the material in the book was swiped from encyclopedias and travel books available in 1356, when it was written, and then embellished.

Another count against it in the truthfulness department: The book is filled with Mandeville's encounters with monsters, dragons, and, as we see pictured here, hound-human hybrids.

But, not to worry! These dog-men and dog-women "be great folk" unless you try to wage war against them: "If they take any man in battle, anon [immediately] they eat him." Well, fair's fair.

Needless to say, the book was extraordinarily popular.[46]

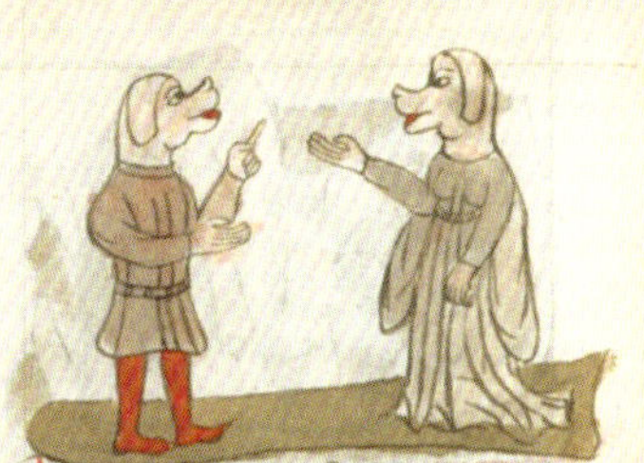

Das sol betüten das sie [illegible] got
lib haben und gen all nackent den
umb die scham tragen sie ein tuch
die sind starck wen sie fechten so
tragen sie ein langen schilt vor
in der bedeckt in den leib und ein
sper in der hand und was sie lüt
vahen die essen sie der kunig vo
der selben insseln ist mechtig und rich
und hatt ein goller an seine hals
von hundert grosser perlein von
orient in der gross als ein hasel
nuss und an dem end ein rain
rubin der ist eins schuchs prait

OKIMONO IN THE FORM OF A PAIR OF GAMBOLING PIEBALD PUPPIES

Japanese, 19th century, porcelain

First things first: We should all use the word "gamboling" a lot more, right?

This statuette featuring gamboling puppies is a Japanese *okimono*, or decorative object.

Okimonos are typically displayed in a *tokonoma*, an alcove used in virtually every Japanese home for showing and contemplating beautiful things.

My *tokonoma* comes from IKEA, and these two silly pups would go straight to the shelf where all my very favorite things live.[47]

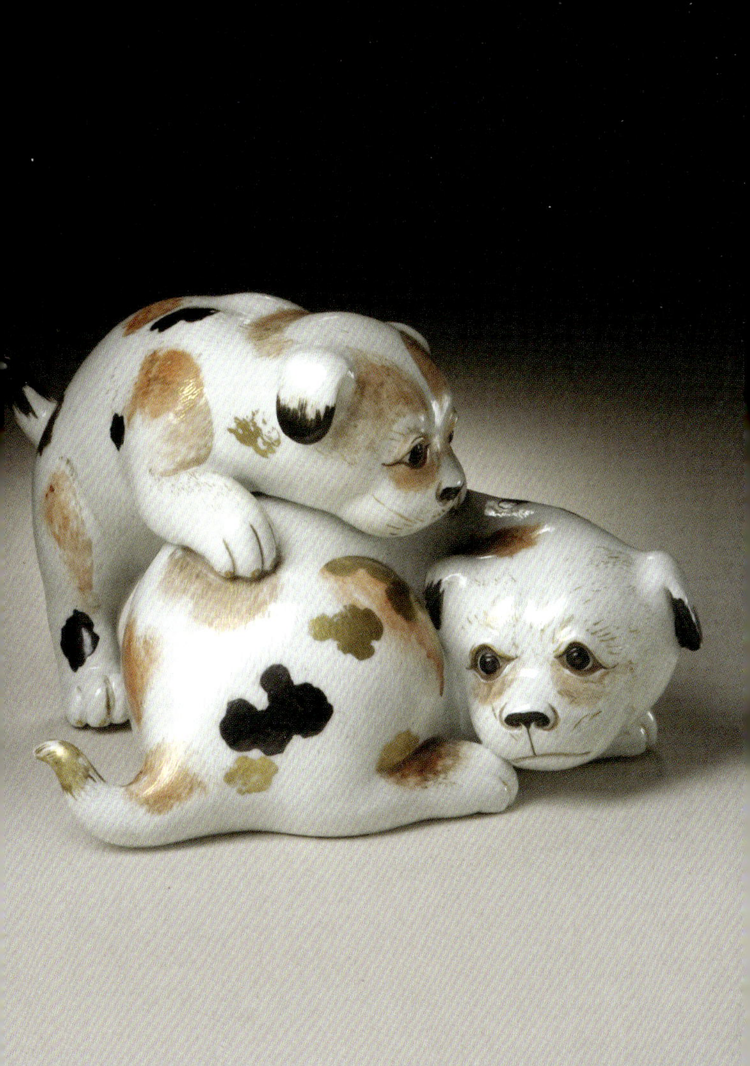

BIRD AND JAPANESE CHIN

Ohara Shōson, Japanese, 1928–1930, woodblock print

Ohara Shōson was regarded as one of the greatest painters in the *kacho-e* (bird-and-flower pictures) tradition.

The bird we see here is a bush warbler, a traditional harbinger of spring. The dog is a Japanese chin, which was typically thought of as elegant and refined. In this picture, the artist, who had an incredible sense of humor (look up his print *Dancing Fox*—a fox on its hind legs with a giant leaf on his head—for additional evidence), has drawn this chin as being ridiculously unaware of the bird or its song.[48]

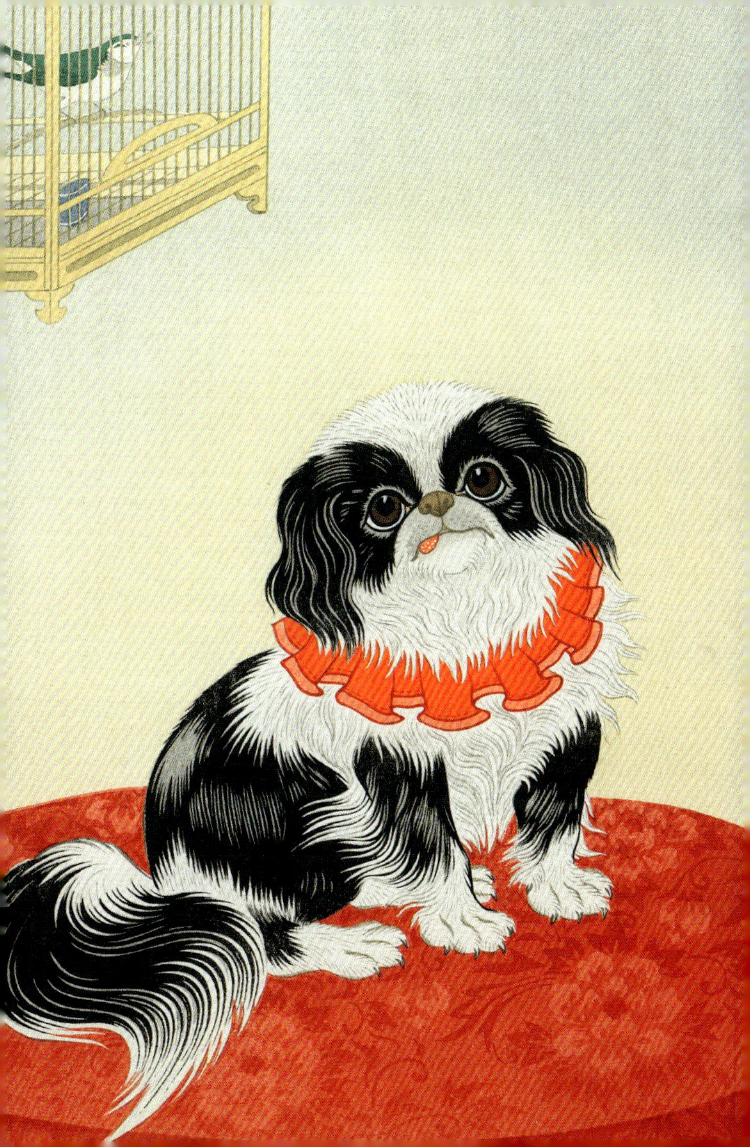

FIREDOG

Attributed to Philippe Caffieri (the Younger), French, ca. 1770, gilt bronze

Wow. Just . . . wow. I think we all need a minute to take in the *audacity* of this object. Okay, you good?

This is one of a pair of firedogs. Non-bonkers versions of firedogs get their name because they look like stick figures of a dog. Typically made of iron, firedogs have four feet that rest on the ground. In a fireplace, firedogs are set a foot or two apart from each other, and the wood is arranged across their backs. This elevates the wood off the floor of the fireplace for better air circulation for the fire.

It's pretty hard to believe this firedog was ever used for practical purposes. Much as I love maximalism, I would not want to have to clean soot off of gold-covered bronze.

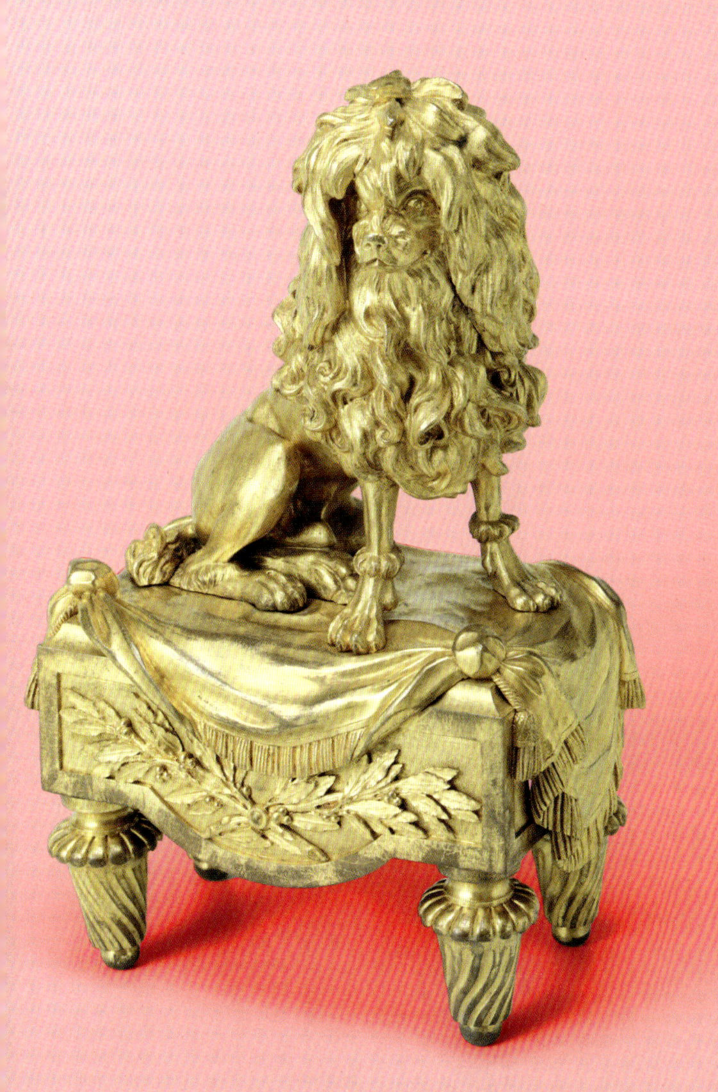

CAESAR AT THE RUBICON

Wilhelm Trübner, German, 1878, oil on canvas

German artist Wilhelm Trübner had a dog named Caesar and a penchant for amusing visual metaphors.

The title of this painting, *Caesar at the Rubicon*, refers to the moment when Julius Caesar paused at the banks of the Rubicon River: Crossing meant starting a civil war, so he wanted to take a beat. Ultimately, he did cross, a decision that led to the eventual fall of the Roman Republic. Oops.

Much like Julius Caesar, Caesar the pup has a decision to make. Snatch the sausage and face the consequences, or be a very good boy? For better or for worse, we'll never know what he chose.

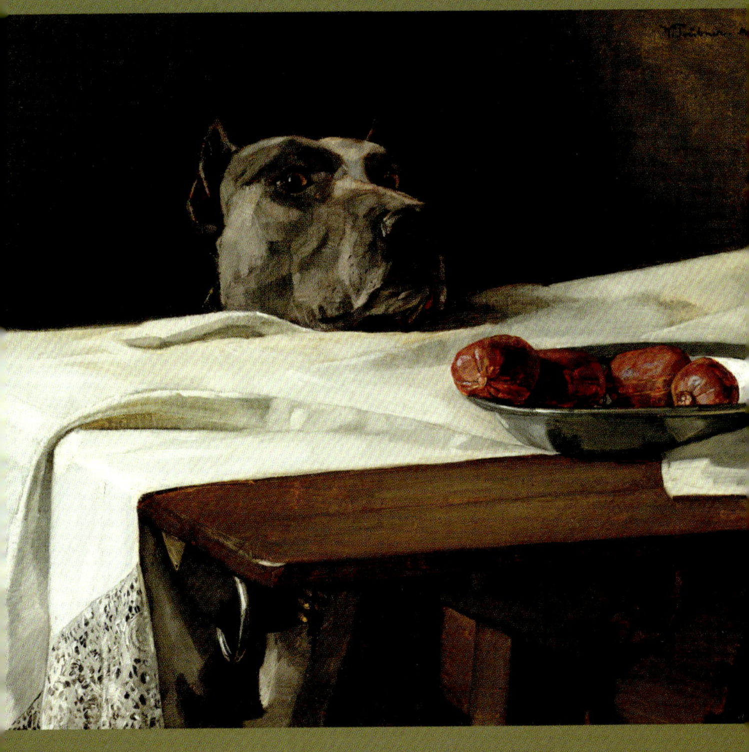

NOTES

1. “Prints from the Korin Gafu (‘Album of Korin Pictures’) and Printed Books from the Nineteenth Century,” RISD Museum, https://risdmuseum.org/exhibitions-events/exhibitions/prints-korin-gafu-album-korin-pictures-and-printed-books-nineteenth.

2. “The Ultimate Historic Guide to British Sweets,” Sweets 4 Me, https://www.sweets4me.co.uk/blogs/our-blog/the-ultimate-historic-guide-to-british-sweets (accessed May 7, 2024).

3. Wikipedia, s.v., “Art Competitions at the 1928 Summer Olympics,” last modified November 22, 2023, https://en.wikipedia.org/wiki/Art_competitions_at_the_1928_Summer_Olympics.

4. Jean Marie Carey, “Eyes Be Closed: Franz Marc’s ‘Liegender Hund im Schnee,’” Textpraxis: Digitales Journal für Philologie 12 (January 2016), https://www.textpraxis.net/jean-marie-carey-eyes-be-closed (accessed May 8, 2024); Susanna Partsch, Franz Marc, and Karen Williams, Franz Marc, 1880–1916 (Germany: Taschen, 2001).

5. Denise Flaim, “Dalmatian History: From Carriage Dogs to Firehouse Mascots,” American Kennel Club, https://www.akc.org/expert-advice/dog-breeds/dalmatian-history/.

6. Wikipedia, s.v., “Order of the Pug,” last modified July 27, 2022, https://en.wikipedia.org/wiki/Order_of_the_Pug.

7. “Lucinda: Nymphenburg Porcelain Manufactory,” Metropolitan Museum of Art, https://www.metmuseum.org/art/collection/search/206291 (accessed May 8, 2024).

8. "The Mystery Ancient Toys Puzzling Archaeologists," BBC, August 16, 2022, https://www.bbc.com/future/article/20220816-the-worlds-oldest-toys-what-toys-were-used-in-the-past; Andrew Smith, "Select Papyri, 1.132: From Diogenis to Alexander," Attalus, February 18, 1921, http://www.attalus.org/docs/select1/p132.html.

9. "Kid's Head," Smithsonian American Art Museum, https://americanart.si.edu/artwork/kids-head-1440 (accessed May 7, 2024).

10. Jasmine G. Gloria, "Connected through Care: Re-Examining the Ceramic Dog Effigies of West Mexico and Peru," master's thesis, University of Colorado, 2022.

11. Teddy Lewis, "Intaglios in the Roman World," Corinium Museum, February 28, 2022.

12. Christine Guth, "Edo: Art in Japan 1615–1868," National Gallery of Art, Washington, D.C., https://www.nga.gov/content/dam/ngaweb/Education/learning-resources/teaching-packets/pdfs/edo-teach.pdf.

13. Joshua J. Mark, "Dogs in Ancient Egypt," World History Encyclopedia, https://www.worldhistory.org/article/1031/dogs-in-ancient-egypt/.

14. Timothy Wilson and Luke Syson, *Maiolica: Italian Renaissance Ceramics in the Metropolitan Museum of Art (Highlights of the Collection)*, Metropolitan Museum of Art.

15. Rebecca Taylor, "A Coin of the Dog Star from Karthaea, Keos," https://blogs.warwick.ac.uk/numismatics/entry/a_coin_of_1/.

16. "Monkey Orchestra," https://www.meissen.com/net/meissencollectiondetail/monkey-orchestra (accessed May 7, 2024).

17. Joshua J. Mark, "Dogs in Ancient Egypt," World History Encyclopedia, https://www.worldhistory.org/article/1031/dogs-in-ancient-egypt/; Melissa M. Thiringer, "An Egyptian's Best Friend? An Analysis and Discussion of the Depiction of the Domestic Dog in Ancient Egypt," master's thesis, University of Memphis, 2020.

18. "Hortensia," Brooklyn Museum, May 7, 2024, https://www.brooklynmuseum.org/eascfa/dinner_party/heritage_floor/hortensia.

19. Louis Trenchard More, *Isaac Newton: A Biography* (London: Charles Scribner's Sons, 1934), https://dn790009.ca.archive.org/0/items/b29977800/b29977800.pdf.

20. Monika Bincsik, "Japanese Incense," Metropolitan Museum of Art, http://www.metmuseum.org/toah/hd/jinc/hd_jinc.html.

21. "Scarab with a Three-Horse Chariot and Driver," Getty Museum Collection, https://www.getty.edu/art/collection/object/103V0X.

22. Wikipedia, s.v., "Western Mexico Shaft Tomb Tradition," last modified December 14, 2023, https://en.wikipedia.org/wiki/Western_Mexico_shaft_tomb_tradition.

23. Heather Colburn Clydesdale, "The Vibrant Role of Mingqi in Early Chinese Burials," in Heilbrunn Timeline of Art History, Metropolitan Museum of Art, 2000–, http://www.metmuseum.org/toah/hd/mgqi/hd_mgqi.htm.

24. "Fact File: Animal Brooches," Vindolanda Charitable Trust, https://www.vindolanda.com/blog/animal-brooches (accessed May 7, 2024).

25. "Confucius Quotes," AZ Quotes, https://www.azquotes.com/quote/524096 (accessed May 7, 2024).

26. "Description and History of Oil Lamps: Roman Oil Lamps Defined," Milwaukee Public Museum, https://www.mpm.edu/research-collections/anthropology/anthropology-collections-research/mediterranean-oil-lamps/description-and-history-oil-lamps (accessed May 7, 2024).

27. Colette Hemingway and Seán Hemingway, "Prehistoric Cypriot Art and Culture," in Heilbrunn Timeline of Art History, Metropolitan Museum of Art, 2000–, http://www.metmuseum.org/toah/hd/pcyp/hd_pcyp.html.

28. "10 Things to Know about Cuypers' Museum Building," Rijksmuseum, https://www.rijksmuseum.nl/en/stories/10-things/story/cuypers-museum-building (accessed May 7, 2024).

29. Joshua J. Mark, "Cosmetics, Perfume, & Hygiene in Ancient Egypt," World History Encyclopedia, https://www.worldhistory.org/article/1061/cosmetics-perfume--hygiene-in-ancient-egypt/ (accessed May 8, 2024).

30. Wikipedia, s.v. "Geremia Discanno," last modified May 22, 2023, https://en.wikipedia.org/wiki/Geremia_Discanno.

31. Wikipedia, s.v., "William James Webbe," last modified April 28, 2023, https://en.wikipedia.org/wiki/William_James_Webbe.

32. Wikipedia, s.v., "Wiener Werkstätte," last modified March 7, 2024, https://en.wikipedia.org/wiki/Wiener_Werkst%C3%A4tte.

33. Stephanie Howard-Smith, "Art Gone to the Dogs: Canine Portraiture in Modern Britain," Art UK, https://artuk.org/discover/stories/art-gone-to-the-dogs-canine-portraiture-in-modern-britain; "Royal Pets: Not Only Corgis," Bridgeman Images, https://blog.bridgemanimages.com/blog/royal-pets-not-corgis.

34. Erik Hinterding, Ernst van de Wetering, and Ger Luijten, *Rembrandt the Printmaker* (London: British Museum Press, 2001).

35. Claude Blair, "Iron: Belgium & Holland," Britannica, https://www.britannica.com/topic/metalwork/Belgium-and-Holland.

36. Zoë Vanderweide, "21 Facts: Gustav Klimt," Sotheby's, https://www.sothebys.com/en/articles/21-facts-gustav-klimt.

37. Maxwell K. Hearn, "The Qing Dynasty (1644–1911): Courtiers, Officials, and Professional Artists," Metropolitan Museum of Art, https://www.metmuseum.org/toah/hd/qing_4/hd_qing_4.html.

38. "Ravegeot et Ravageole, Chiens Bassets," Silla Antiques & Art, https://www.sillafineantiques.com/ravegeot-et-ravageole-chiens-bassets-emmanuel-fremiet/ (accessed May 7, 2024); Wikipedia, s.v., "Emmanuel Frémiet," last modified December 20, 2023, https://en.wikipedia.org/wiki/Emmanuel_Fr%C3%A9miet.

39. D. Krugner, "Buttons—A History," Western Regional Button Association, https://wrba.us/ref-library/about-buttons/buttons-a-history/.

40. Ricky Jay, *Jay's Journal of Anomalies: Conjurers, Cheats, Hustlers, Hoaxsters, Pranksters, Jokesters, Imposters, Pretenders, Side-Show Showmen, Armless Calligraphers, Mechanical Marvels, Popular Entertainments* (New York: Farrar, Straus and Giroux, 2001).

41. Naomi Daw, "The Parting Starts after Eight: A Stirrup Cup in the Willett Collection of Popular Pottery," Brighton & Hove Museums, https://brightonmuseums.org.uk/discovery/history-stories/the-parting-starts-after-eight-a-stirrup-cup-in-the-willett-collection-of-popular-pottery/ (accessed May 7, 2024).

42. Sarah Lees, *Nineteenth-Century European Paintings at the Sterling and Francine Clark Art Institute*, Vol.2 (New Haven, CT: Yale University Press, 2012), https://media.clarkart.edu/1955.597_EuroCat.pdf.

43. Cindy Kang, "Auguste Renoir (1841–1919)," Metropolitan Museum of Art, https://www.metmuseum.org/toah/hd/augu/hd_augu.html; Margaret Samu, "Impressionism: Art and Modernity," Metropolitan Museum of Art, https://www.metmuseum.org/toah/hd/imml/hd_imml.html.

44. "Urania's Mirror; or, a View of the Heavens (Circa 1825)," Public Domain Review, https://publicdomainreview.org/collection/uranias-mirror-or-a-view-of-the-heavens/.

45. Wikipedia, s.v., "Akan Goldweights," last modified April 14, 2024, https://en.wikipedia.org/wiki/Akan_goldweights; Wikipedia, s.v., "Abusua," last modified May 2, 2024, https://en.wikipedia.org/wiki/Abusua.

46. *The Travels of Sir John Mandeville* (London: Macmillan and Co., 1900), https://www.gutenberg.org/files/782/782-h/782-h.htm.

47. Elizabeth Dawson, "History of Okimono," Okimono Project, https://okimonoproject.wordpress.com/2014/11/01/history-of-the-okimonos-2/.

48. "Japanese Chin History: Japan's Royal Spaniel," American Kennel Club, https://www.akc.org/expert-advice/dog-breeds/japanese-chin-history-japans-royal-spaniel/.

IMAGE CREDITS

Bronze Statuette of a Hound Gnawing a Bone, 3rd–2nd century BC, Bronze, 3 in. (7.6 cm), Fletcher Fund, 1936, Metropolitan Museum of Art, New York, https://www.metmuseum.org/art/collection/search/253516

Nakamura Hôchû, 1826, Three Young Dogs, Paper, 256 × 367 mm, Rijksmuseum, Amsterdam, Netherlands, http://hdl.handle.net/10934/RM0001.COLLECT.346037

Sketch of a Dog, ca. 1295–1070 BC, Limestone and ink, H $2\frac{13}{16}$ × W $3\frac{3}{4}$ × Th. $\frac{9}{16}$ in. (7.1 × 9.6 × 1.5 cm), Gift of Theodore M. Davis, New York, 1914, Metropolitan Museum of Art, New York, https://www.metmuseum.org/art/collection/search/548233

Box, early 19th century, Enamel on copper, $1\frac{5}{8}$ × $1\frac{5}{8}$ × $1\frac{1}{4}$ in. (4.1 × 4.1 × 3.2 cm), Gift of Louise Knobloch, 1966, The Metropolitan Museum of Art, New York, https://www.metmuseum.org/art/collection/search/204628

Dog Pendant, 1575–1600, Gold, rubies, pearls, and enamel, H. 3 in. (7.5 cm), Smithsonian American Art Museum, Gift of John Gellatly, https://www.si.edu/object/pendant:saam_1929.8.194

Dog Sled with Three Dogs, late 19th century, Walrus ivory, pigment, string, and animal hide, $1\frac{5}{16}$ × $1\frac{1}{4}$ × 5 in. (3.33 × 3.18 × 12.7 cm) (sled only), Minneapolis Institute of Art, Minneapolis, Minnesota, https://collections.artsmia.org/art/80216/dog-sled-with-three-dogs-inuit

Bertha van Hasselt, 1930, Sleeping Dog, Paper, 320 × 435 mm, Rijksmuseum, Amsterdam, Netherlands, http://hdl.handle.net/10934/RM0001.COLLECT.206954

Poodle Powder Box, 1940, Graphite pencil, ink, gouache, and tracing paper, 15.2 cm × 10.8 cm, Petit Palais, Museum of Fine Arts of the City of Paris, https://www.parismuseescollections.paris.fr/fr/petit-palais/oeuvres/poudrier-caniches#infos-principales

Bolognese Terrier, 1811–50, Hard-paste porcelain, $8\frac{7}{8}$ × $12\frac{3}{8}$ in. (22.5 × 31.4 cm), Metropolitan Museum of Art, The Charles E. Sampson Memorial Fund, 1969, New York, https://www.metmuseum.org/art/collection/search/205132

Single Spout and Bridge Vessel in the Form of a Dog Gnawing a Bone, 700–1000, Ceramic and pigment, $4\frac{1}{2}$ × $6\frac{3}{8}$ in., Art Institute of Chicago, https://www.artic.edu/artworks/91456/single-spout-and-bridge-vessel-in-the-form-of-a-dog-gnawing-a-bone

Spectacle Case, late 19th century, Glass beads, linen, leather, and metal, Gift of the Brooklyn Museum, 2009; Gift of Dwight W. Morrow, Jr., Constance Morrow Morgan, and Anne Morrow Lindbergh, 1956, Brooklyn Museum Costume Collection at the Metropolitan Museum of Art, New York, https://www.metmuseum.org/art/collection/search/156670

Netsuke of Dog on a Stand, 19th century, Red lacquer, H. $1\frac{1}{2}$ in. (3.8 cm); W. 1 in. square (2.5 cm), Gift of Mrs. Russell Sage, 1910, Metropolitan Museum of Art, New York, https://www.metmuseum.org/art/collection/search/59063

Franz Marc, 1909–1910, Siberian Dogs in the Snow, Oil on canvas, 80.5 × 114 cm ($31\frac{11}{16}$ × $44\frac{7}{8}$ in.), National Gallery of Art, Washington, D.C., https://www.nga.gov/collection/art-object-page.62640.html

Dog, late 17th century, Porcelain with overglaze enamels (Hizen ware, Kakiemon type), H. $6\frac{1}{4}$ in. (15.9 cm); W. $6\frac{1}{4}$ in. (15.9 cm); L. $8\frac{7}{8}$ in. (22.5 cm), The Harry G. C. Packard Collection of Asian Art, Gift of Harry G. C. Packard, and Purchase, Fletcher, Rogers, Harris Brisbane Dick, and Louis V. Bell Funds, Joseph Pulitzer Bequest, and The Annenberg Fund Inc. Gift, 1975, Metropolitan Museum of Art, New York, https://www.metmuseum.org/art/collection/search/57156

Dalmatian, 20th century, Carved and painted wood with metal and resin, $13\frac{3}{4}$ × $20\frac{1}{8}$ × 6 in. (34.9 × 51.2 × 15.2 cm), Smithsonian American Art Museum and its Renwick Gallery, Washington, D.C., https://www.si.edu/object/dalmatian:saam_1986.65.292

Lid, 5th century BC, Bronze, 12.5 × 22.6 cm ($4\frac{15}{16}$ × $8\frac{7}{8}$ in.), The Getty Center, Los Angeles, https://www.getty.edu/art/collection/object/103SSW

Z. S. Lupus, Dog (Mantel Ornament), ca. 1938, Watercolor and graphite on paperboard, 28.5 × 21.6 cm ($11\frac{1}{4}$ × $8\frac{1}{2}$ in.), National Gallery of Art, Washington, D.C., https://www.nga.gov/collection/art-object-page.20483.html

Figure of a Poodle, 1820–40, Glazed and hand-painted earthenware, 6.7 × 4.3 × 3 cm ($2\frac{5}{8}$ × $1\frac{11}{16}$ × $1\frac{3}{16}$ in.), Cooper Hewitt, Smithsonian Design Museum Collection, New York, https://www.si.edu/object/figure-poodle:chndm_1992-5-21

Pendant, 14th century, Champlevé enamel, copper, and gilt, $2\frac{13}{16}$ × $2\frac{3}{8}$ × $\frac{1}{4}$ in. (7.2 × 6 × 0.7 cm), Gift of J. Pierpont Morgan, 1917, Metropolitan Museum of Art, New York, https://www.metmuseum.org/art/collection/search/464665

The Pug Lady, 1744–1750, Hard porcelain, enamel (ceramic technique), 28 cm × 21 cm × 14.5 cm, Petit Palais, Museum of Fine Arts of the City of Paris, https://www.parismuseescollections.paris.fr/fr/petit-palais/oeuvres/la-dame-aux-carlins#infos-principales

Apulian Dog Head Rhyton, 340–330 BC, Terracotta, 19.5 × 9.3 cm ($7\frac{11}{16}$ × $3\frac{11}{16}$ in.), The Getty Center, Los Angeles, CA, https://www.getty.edu/art/collection/object/103SSQ#full-artwork-details

Musette, a Maltese dog, 1855–68, Hard-paste porcelain, H. $15\frac{1}{2}$ in. (39.4 cm), The Charles E. Sampson Memorial Fund, 1977, The Metropolitan Museum of Art, New York, https://www.metmuseum.org/art/collection/search/206595

Dog, ca. AD 100–300, Clay, $9\frac{1}{2}$ × $6\frac{1}{16}$ × $13\frac{1}{16}$ in. (24.1 × 15.4 × 33.2 cm), Gift of Dr. and Mrs. John R. Kennedy, Minneapolis Institute of Art, Minneapolis, Minnesota, https://collections.artsmia.org/art/5992/dog-colima

Pieter van Somerwil, Doghouse, 1773, Silver, H. 2.7 cm × W. 4.4 cm × D. 3.8 cm, weight 26.39 g, Rijksmuseum, Amsterdam, Netherlands, http://hdl.handle .net/10934/RM0001.COLLECT.230697

Pair of Spaniels, ca. 1830–50, Lead-glazed earthenware with copper lustre embellishments, H. (each) 9¼ in. (23.5 cm), Gift of Sidney H. and Helen M. Witty, 1976, Metropolitan Museum of Art, New York, https://www.metmuseum .org/art/collection/search/206567

Franz Anton Bustelli, Dog, Nymphenburg Porcelain Manufactory, ca. 1760, Hard-paste porcelain, H. 11.6 cm × W. 16 cm, Rijksmuseum, Amsterdam, Netherlands, http://hdl.handle.net/10934/RM0001.COLLECT.60871

Inkstand, ca. 1530–50, Bronze, Overall (with base) 4⅜ × 2¾ in. (11.1 × 7 cm); H. (without base) 3 in. (7.6 cm), Gift of Ogden Mills, 1927, Metropolitan Museum of Art New York, https://www.metmuseum.org/art/collection/search/195728

Toy Dog, ca. 1550–1292 BC (New Kingdom), Ebony, H. $1\frac{7}{16}$ × L. 2⅞ in. (3.7 × 7.3 cm), Acquired by Henry Walters, The Walters Art Museum, Baltimore, Maryland, 1911, https://art.thewalters.org/detail/39978/toy-dog/

Paul Wayland Bartlett, Sleeping Dog, ca. 1880–1895?, Plaster, 1⅜ × 3 × 2¼ in. (3.6 × 7.6 × 5.7 cm), Smithsonian American Art Museum and its Renwick Gallery, https://www.si.edu/object/sleeping-dog:saam_1971.458

Leaping Dog, 18th century, Glass, lampwork (verre de Nevers), metal armature, H. 5.7 cm (2¼ in.), Gift of Mrs. Potter Palmer, Art Institute of Chicago, https:// www.artic.edu/artworks/52523/leaping-dog

Dogs Playing, 200 BC–AD 500, Unslipped buff ceramic with incised decoration, 3⅛ × 4⅜ in. (7.94 × 11.11 cm), Los Angeles County Museum of Art, Los Angeles, https://collections.lacma.org/node/253747

Textile Fragment with Repeating Pattern of Dogs on Dotted Ground, 18th–19th century, Silk, L. 6¼ in. (15.88 cm); W. 5 in. (12.70 cm), Gift of Mr. and Mrs. H. O. Havemeyer, 1896, The Metropolitan Museum of Art, New York, https://www .metmuseum.org/art/collection/search/65886

Dog with Orange Bib, 1615–1868, Paulownia wood, gofun (ground shell white), silk, and pigments, 7¾ × 5¼ × 7¼ in. (19.69 × 13.34 × 18.42 cm), Gift of Mrs. Charlene S. Kornblum and Dr. S. Sanford Kornblum (M.2017.41), Los Angeles County Museum of Art, Los Angeles, https://collections.lacma.org/ node/2255428

Carved Intaglio Gemstone with a Running and Barking Dog, 1st–2nd century AD, Carnelian, $\frac{7}{16}$ × ⅜ × ⅛ in. (1.1 × 1 × 0.3 cm), Accession Number 1986.17.7, Gift of Ambassador and Mrs. William L. Eagleton, Jr., B.A., 1948, Yale University Art Gallery, New Haven, Connecticut, https://artgallery.yale.edu/collections/ objects/57830

Puppy, 19th century, Bronze, 18 × 48 × 48 cm, Cernuschi Museum, Museum of Asian Arts of the City of Paris, https://www.parismuseescollections.paris.fr/fr/ musee-cernuschi/oeuvres/chiot#infos-principales

Terracotta Askos in the Form of a Dog, 2nd–1st century BC, Terracotta, H. 3 9/16 in. (9.1 cm); W. 4 7/16 in. (11.3 cm), The Metropolitan Museum of Art, New York, https://www.metmuseum.org/art/collection/search/256597

Émile Gallé, Figure of a Dog, 1870–80, Glazed earthenware, H × W × D: 30.7 × 17 × 23.1 cm (12 1/16 × 6 11/16 × 9 1/8 in.), Cooper Hewitt, Gift of Anonymous Donor, Smithsonian Design Museum, New York, https://www.si.edu/object/figure-dog:chndm_1967-48-108

Game of Hounds and Jackals, ca. 1814–1805 BC, Ebony, ivory, Purchase, Edward S. Harkness Gift, 1926 (26.7.1287a-k); Gift of Lord Carnarvon, 2012 (2012.508), The Metropolitan Museum of Art, New York

Double-Sided Votive Relief, 305–30 BC, Limestone, 8.3 × 6.5 × 1.4 cm (3 1/4 × 2 9/16 × 9/16 in.), Gift of the John Huntington Art and Polytechnic Trust 1914.666.b, The Cleveland Museum of Art, Cleveland, Ohio, https://www.clevelandart.org/art/1914.666.b

Dog, 1590–1610, Majolica, H. 8 cm, D. 27.2 cm, Petit Palais, Museum of Fine Arts of the City of Paris, https://www.parismuseescollections.paris.fr/fr/petit-palais/oeuvres/chien#infos-principales

Greek Terracotta Statue Dog, 500–475 BC, terracotta, 11.3 cm, Collection Loeb, SL 120, Katalog Nr. 46, Photograph by Matthias Kabel, https://commons.wikimedia.org/wiki/File:Greek_terracotta_statue_dog_with_pray_Staatliche_Antikensammlungen_SL_120.jpg

Ring, 4th century BC, Silver, object (bezel): 1 × 0.8 cm (3/8 × 5/16 in.), Object (Hoop, Greatest Extent): 1.9 cm (3/4 in.), The Getty Center, Los Angeles, https://www.getty.edu/art/collection/object/1062PW?altImage=7e3ca82d-ac96-4b6b-8432-f203d9799ec5

Johann Joachim Kändler, Hunting Dog Scratching, ca. 1755, Porcelain, H. 4 cm, W. 5 cm, D. 4 cm, Cognacq-Jay Museum, Paris, France, https://www.parismuseescollections.paris.fr/fr/musee-cognacq-jay/oeuvres/chien-de-chasse-se-grattant#infos-principales

Dog Game Piece, ca. 2850 BC, Hippopotamus ivory, 1 3/16 × 2 9/16 × 13/16 in. (3 × 6.5 × 2.1 cm), Acquired by Henry Walters, 1913, The Walters Art Museum, Baltimore, Maryland, https://art.thewalters.org/detail/40159/dog-game-piece/

Roman Dog Brooch, 100–200, Copper alloy, 45.4 mm × 22.5 mm × 16mm, Portable Antiquities Scheme, The British Museum, London, https://finds.org.uk/database/artefacts/record/id/117750

Pipe Tamper (Unique ID HESH-AC&226), 1650–1750, Copper alloy, 40.1 mm × 17.1 mm × 7.4 mm, Portable Antiquities Scheme, The British Museum, London, https://finds.org.uk/database/artefacts/record/id/32927

Pipe Tamper (Unique ID ESS-4BE896), 1650–1850, 20.93 × 25.03 × 5.02 mm, Portable Antiquities Scheme, The British Museum, London, https://finds.org.uk/database/artefacts/record/id/705644

Pipe Tamper (Unique ID NMS-5FFCE1), 1650–1800, 21 × 29.5 × 7 mm, Portable Antiquities Scheme, The British Museum, London, https://finds.org.uk/database/artefacts/record/id/461094

Incense Burner in the Form of a Dog, ca. 1750–1800, Porcelain, underglaze blue, $5\frac{1}{8}$ × $3\frac{7}{8}$ × $5\frac{1}{4}$ in. (13 × 9.8 × 13.3 cm), The Walters Art Museum, Baltimore, Maryland, https://art.thewalters.org/detail/6281/incense-burner-koro-in-form-of-a-dog/

Scarab, 4th–3rd century BC, Cornelian, 1.6 × 1.2 × 0.9 cm ($\frac{5}{8}$ × $\frac{1}{2}$ × $\frac{3}{8}$ in.), The Getty Center, Los Angeles, https://www.getty.edu/art/collection/object/103XAT#full-artwork-details

Joined Dogs, 200 BC–AD 500, Slip-painted ceramic, $4\frac{1}{2}$ × $6\frac{1}{4}$ × $4\frac{1}{2}$ in. (11.43 × 15.88 × 11.43 cm), Los Angeles County Museum of Art, Los Angeles, https://collections.lacma.org/node/253567

Dog, 902–979, Sandstone and celadon, 5.7 × 9.4 × 4.4 cm, Cernuschi Museum, Museum of Asian Arts of the City of Paris, https://www.parismuseescollections.paris.fr/fr/musee-cernuschi/oeuvres/chien-11#infos-principales

Netsuke of Seated Puppy with Short Curled Tail, Wood and gold lacquer, $1\frac{1}{8}$ in. (2.9 cm) × 1 in. (2.5 cm) × $1\frac{1}{2}$ in. (3.8 cm), The Metropolitan Museum of Art, New York, https://www.metmuseum.org/art/collection/search/59623

Figure of a Recumbent Dog, 6th century, Gray earthenware with red polychrome, $3\frac{5}{8}$ × $6\frac{1}{4}$ × $3\frac{5}{8}$ in. (9.2 × 15.8 × 9.2 cm), Gift of the Guennol Collection, Brooklyn Museum, Brooklyn, New York, https://www.brooklynmuseum.org/opencollection/objects/159018

Edwin Landseer, Dog Resting Upon a Couch, 1817, Pencil, H × W: 14.1 × 20 cm ($5\frac{9}{16}$ × $8\frac{1}{8}$ in.), RISD Museum, Museum Works of Art Fund 72.022, Providence, Rhode Island, https://risdmuseum.org/art-design/collection/dog-resting-upon-couch-72022

Brooch, AD 75–199, Copper alloy, 43 × 18 mm, Portable Antiquities Scheme, The British Museum, London, https://finds.org.uk/database/artefacts/record/id/524001

Seated Dog, 386–535, Earthenware, D. $4\frac{1}{4}$ in., Bequest of Alfred F. Pillsbury, Minneapolis Institute of Art, Minneapolis, Minnesota, https://collections.artsmia.org/art/872/seated-dog-china

Lamp, 1st–4th century, Terracotta, 6.3 × 7.1 × 12.2 cm ($2\frac{1}{2}$ × $2\frac{13}{16}$ × $4\frac{13}{16}$ in.), The Getty Center, Los Angeles, https://www.getty.edu/art/collection/object/103YOY

Pug Dog, 18th century, Ceramic, hard porcelain, and enamel (ceramic technique), 15 × 14.5 × 7.5 cm, Donation of Edward and Julia Tuck, Petit Palais, Museum of Fine Arts of the City of Paris, https://www.parismuseescollections.paris.fr/fr/petit-palais/oeuvres/chien-carlin#infos-principales

Pug Dog Nursing Her Puppy, Ceramic, hard porcelain, and enamel (ceramic technique), 15.5 × 13.5 × 7.5 cm, Donation of Edward and Julia Tuck, Petit Palais, Museum of Fine Arts of the City of Paris, https://www.parismuseescollections.paris.fr/fr/petit-palais/oeuvres/chienne-carlin-allaitant-son-petit#infos-principales

Limestone Dog, 4th–3rd century BC, Limestone, 17¾ × 6⅜ × 11 in., 42 lb. (45.1 × 16.2 × 27.9 cm, 19.1 kg), The Cesnola Collection, Purchased by subscription, 1874–76, The Metropolitan Museum of Art, New York, https://www.metmuseum.org/art/collection/search/242174

Waterspout Fragment in the Shape of a Dog, 1st century BC, Terracotta, 15.6 cm (6⅛ in.), The Getty Center, Los Angeles, https://www.getty.edu/art/collection/object/103SWF

Dog, 1271–1368, Jade, Cultural relics drawing number K1C002194N-000000000PAB, National Palace Museum, Taipei City, Taiwan, https://theme.npm.edu.tw/opendata/DigitImageSets.aspx?sNo=04009857

Dog in Feathered Hat and Ruffled Collar Match Safe, Silver, 5.9 × 2.7 × 1.5 cm (2 5/16 × 11/16 × 9/16 in.), Gift of Stephen W. Brener and Carol B. Brener, Cooper Hewitt, Smithsonian Design Museum, New York, https://collection.cooperhewitt.org/objects/18533709/with-image-9722/

Eduard Cuypers, late 19th century, Dog's Head, Etching, paper, chine collé, plate edge, H. 116 mm × W. 77 mm, Rijksmuseum, Amsterdam, Netherlands, http://hdl.handle.net/10934/RM0001.COLLECT.203180

John Frederick Herring, 1855, A Hound and a Bearded Collie Seated on a Hunting Coat, Oil on paper laid on canvas, 9¾ × 13½ in. (24.8 × 34.3 cm), Yale Center for British Art, Paul Mellon Collection, New Haven, Connecticut, https://collections.britishart.yale.edu/catalog/tms:54299

Cosmetic Dish in the Shape of a Dog, ca. 1550–1295 BC, Bone, L. 9.7 cm (3 13/16 in.); W. 2.7 cm (1 1/16 in.); H. 0.9 cm (⅜ in.) Th. at head 0.6 cm (¼ in.), Gift of Helen Miller Gould, 1910, The Metropolitan Museum of Art, New York, https://www.metmuseum.org/art/collection/search/545210

Johannes Mock, after Mansfeld, 1825, Dog's Head with a Collar and Ring, Paper, plate edge, H. 106 mm × W. 155 mm, Rijksmuseum, Amsterdam, Netherlands, http://hdl.handle.net/10934/RM0001.COLLECT.154921

Geremia Discanno, 1882, Mosaic in House of L Caecilius Iucundus Pompeii by Geremia Discanno, Paper, https://commons.wikimedia.org/wiki/File:Mosaic_in_House_of_L_Caecilius_Jucundus_Pompeii_by_Gerremia_Discanno_pub_1882.jpg

Henri-Charles Guérard, 1870–1887, Azor, paper, 7 5/16 × 6⅞ in. (20.1 × 17.5 cm), The Miriam and Ira D. Wallach Division of Art, Prints and Photographs: Print Collection, The New York Public Library, New York, https://digitalcollections.nypl.org/items/b0b1aaf0-1f94-0134-aac6-00505686a51c

Otto Eerelman, ca. 1880–1892, Head of a Leonberger, Paper, chalk, and watercolor, 648 × 498 mm, Rijksmuseum, Amsterdam, Netherlands, http://hdl.handle.net/10934/RM0001.COLLECT.304208

William Webbe, ca. 1825, A Blenheim Spaniel, Oil on canvas, $25\frac{1}{2}$ × 29 in. (64.8 × 73.7 cm), Yale Center for British Art, New Haven, Connecticut, https://collections.britishart.yale.edu/catalog/tms:1131

Bronze Statuette of a Dog, 2nd–3rd century, Bronze, H. $3\frac{3}{8}$ in. (8.6 cm), Edith Perry Chapman Fund, New York, 1962, Metropolitan Museum of Art, https://www.metmuseum.org/art/collection/search/255121

Moriz Jung, 1912, Postcard from the Wiener Werkstätte No. 677: Greyhound, Paperboard, 14.1 × 8.9 cm, Wien Museum, Vienna, Austria, https://sammlung.wienmuseum.at/en/object/179084/

After Edwin Henry Landseer (artist) and Thomas Landseer (engraver), 1844, The Lion-Dog of Malta—The Last of His Tribe, Mixed method engraving on chine collé; proof before letters, $19\frac{1}{2}$ × $22\frac{1}{16}$ in. (49.5 × 56 cm); sheet $20\frac{7}{8}$ × $25\frac{3}{8}$ in. (53 × 64.5 cm), The Metropolitan Museum of Art, New York, https://www.metmuseum.org/art/collection/search/655905

Rembrandt van Rijn, ca. 1640, Sleeping Dog, Paper, H. 39 mm × W. 81 mm, Rijksmuseum, Amsterdam, Netherlands, http://hdl.handle.net/10934/RM0001.COLLECT.36292

Henri de Toulouse-Lautrec, n.d., Two Dogs, Pen and ink on paper, $2\frac{15}{16}$ × $8\frac{1}{4}$ in. (7.5 × 21 cm), $2\frac{15}{16}$ × $8\frac{1}{4}$ in. (7.5 × 21 cm), Bequest of Gregoire Tarnopol, 1979, and Gift of Alexander Tarnopol, 1980, The Metropolitan Museum of Art, New York, https://www.metmuseum.org/art/collection/search/334355

Wenceslaus Hollar, 1647, Six Reclining Hunting Dogs, Paper, plate edge, H. 140 mm × W. 205 mm, Rijksmuseum, Amsterdam, Netherlands, http://hdl.handle.net/10934/RM0001.COLLECT.32845

Door Knocker in the Shape of a Small Dog, 15th or 16th century, Wrought iron, without tang, $71\frac{1}{16}$ × $1\frac{7}{8}$ × $22\frac{1}{8}$ in. (18 × 4.7 × 5.4 cm), Overall, with mounting (tang): $7\frac{1}{16}$ × $1\frac{7}{8}$ × $3\frac{15}{16}$ in. (18 × 4.7 × 10 cm), The Cloisters Collection, 2016, The Metropolitan Museum of Art, New York, https://www.metmuseum.org/art/collection/search/712742

Hunting Dog, 15th–16th century or later, Wrought iron, overall: $6\frac{7}{8}$ × $\frac{9}{16}$ × 1 in. (17.5 × 4 × 2.5 cm); with mount: $8\frac{1}{16}$ × $10\frac{1}{16}$ × $2\frac{7}{16}$ in. (20.5 × 25.6 × 6.2 cm), The Metropolitan Museum of Art, New York, https://www.metmuseum.org/art/collection/search/468493

Gustav Klimt, 1902–1904, Two Studies of a Poodle, Packing paper, 44.2 × 31.7 cm, Wien Museum, Vienna, Austria, https://sammlung.wienmuseum.at/en/object/162762-zwei-studien-zu-einem-pudel/

Amulet of a Dog, 2123–2040 BC, Turquoise-green faience, 1 cm ($\frac{3}{8}$ in.), Cleveland Museum of Art, Cleveland, Ohio, https://www.clevelandart.org/art/1914.793.6#

Incense Boxes in the Shape of Dog Charms, ca. 1840, Porcelain with overglaze enamels (Minpei kilns), H. 1¾ in. (4.4 cm); L. 2½ in. (6.4 cm), The Metropolitan Museum of Art, New York, https://www.metmuseum.org/art/collection/search/45358 and https://www.metmuseum.org/art/collection/search/45359

Hound, 19th–20th century, Porcelain, The Walters Art Museum, Baltimore, Maryland, https://art.thewalters.org/detail/21963/hound/

Stick Pin with Hound's Head, 1870s, Gold, lapis lazuli, enamel, H. 3⅛ × W. 1/16 in. (7.9 × 0.19 cm), The Walters Art Museum, Baltimore, Maryland, https://art.thewalters.org/detail/6203/stick-pin-with-hounds-head/

Giuseppe Castiglione, One of Ten Noble Dogs, Named Mo-yu Ch'ih, Qing dynasty, Painting, 247.5 × 164.4 mm, National Palace Museum, Taipei City, Taiwan, https://theme.npm.edu.tw/opendata/DigitImageSets.aspx?sNo=04024411&lang=2&Key=dog&pageNo=3

Julie de Graag, 1917, Dog, Paper, H. 153 mm × W. 188 mm, Rijksmuseum, Amsterdam, Netherlands, https://www.rijksmuseum.nl/nl/collectie/RP-P-1935-890

Emmanuel Frémiet, 19th century, Dog Study, Graphite pencil and paper, 19.1 × 9 cm, Petit Palais, Museum of Fine Arts of the City of Paris, https://www.parismuseescollections.paris.fr/fr/petit-palais/oeuvres/etude-de-chien-1#infos-secondaires-detail

Emmanuel Frémiet, 1853, Two Seated Basset Hounds, Bronze, H. 13.97 cm (5½ in.), National Gallery of Art, Washington, D.C., https://www.nga.gov/collection/art-object-page.164922.html

Nicolas-Toussaint Charlet, Pointer Dog Head, 1828, Lithography, 25.5 × 35.3 cm, Carnavalet Museum, History of Paris, https://www.parismuseescollections.paris.fr/fr/musee-carnavalet/oeuvres/tete-de-chien-braque-9#infos-principales

White Porcelain Button, Painted with a Dog, undated, Porcelain, Carnavalet Museum, History of Paris, https://www.parismuse scollections.paris.fr/fr/musee-carnavalet/oeuvres/bouton-en-porcelaine-blanche-peint-avec-un-chien#infos-secondaires-detail

Jean-Pierre Dantan, 1840, Statuette of Munito the Poodle, Bronze, 18 cm, Carnavalet Museum, History of Paris, https://www.parismuseescollections.paris.fr/fr/musee-carnavalet/oeuvres/statuette-du-chien-caniche-munito#infos-principales

Dog Head Stirrup Cup, 1810–20, Ceramic and earthenware, 2½ × 5 × 4 in (6.35 × 12.7 × 10.16 cm), National Museum of American History, Washington, D.C., https://www.si.edu/object/dog-head-stirrup-cup:nmah_577468

Auguste Renoir, ca. 1876, Tama, the Japanese Dog, Oil on canvas, 15 1/16 × 18 3/16 in. (38.3 × 46.2 cm); Frame: 21 × 24 3/16 in. (53.3 × 61.4 cm), The Clark Museum, Williamstown, Massachusetts, https://www.clarkart.edu/ArtPiece/Detail/Tama,-the-Japanese-Dog-(1)

Édouard Manet, ca. 1875, Tama, the Japanese Dog, Oil on canvas, 61 × 50 cm (24 × 19$\frac{11}{16}$ in.), National Gallery of Art, Washington, D.C., https://www.nga.gov/collection/art-object-page.92997.html

Totoya Hokkei, ca. 1825, Puppy with a Slice of Dried Salmon, Surimono, shikishi-ban, Polychrome woodblock print with light gauffrage, 8$\frac{7}{16}$ × 7$\frac{5}{16}$ in. (21.5 × 18.5 cm), Gift of Virginia Shawan Drosten and Patrick Kenadjian, B.A. 1970, Yale University Art Gallery, New Haven, Connecticut, https://artgallery.yale.edu/collections/objects/160596

Auguste Renoir, 1870, Head of a Dog, Oil on canvas, 21.9 × 20 cm (8$\frac{5}{8}$ × 7$\frac{7}{8}$ in.), Ailsa Mellon Bruce Collection, National Gallery of Art, Washington, D.C., https://www.nga.gov/collection/art-object-page.52201.html

Sidney Hall, 1825, Canis Major, Illustration in Urania's Mirror, pl. 30., Print on layered paper board: etching, hand-colored, Library of Congress, Washington, D.C., https://www.loc.gov/pictures/item/2002695520/

Gold-Weight (Abrammuo): Dog, 19th century, Brass, H. 2.5 cm, W. 3.8 cm, D. 1.9 cm (1 × 1$\frac{1}{2}$ × $\frac{3}{4}$ in.), Princeton University Art Museum, https://artmuseum.princeton.edu/collections/objects/31083

Travels of Sir John Mandeville, 1459, Drawings on paper, 1–170v, 212 × 153 mm, Spencer Collection, The New York Public Library, New York, https://digitalcollections.nypl.org/items/5824a190-6516-013a-a95c-0242ac110003

Okimono in the Form of a Pair of Gamboling Piebald Puppies, 19th century, Porcelain, 5$\frac{3}{8}$ × 10$\frac{1}{16}$ × 8$\frac{1}{8}$ in. (13.6 × 25.5 × 20.5 cm), Gift of Allan and Maxine Kurtzman (AC1998.115.25), Los Angeles County Museum of Art, Los Angeles, https://collections.lacma.org/node/189958

Ohara Shōson, ca. 1928–1930, Pug Dog, Woodblock print; ink and color on paper, 13 × 9$\frac{7}{16}$ in. (33 × 24 cm), Gift of Paul Schweitzer, Minneapolis Institute of Art, Minneapolis, Minnesota, https://collections.artsmia.org/art/91678/pug-dog-ohara-shoson

Philippe Caffieri (the Younger), ca. 1770, Pair of Firedogs, Bronze (metal), gilding (material), H. 39.1 cm × W. 25.1 cm × D. 15 cm, Rijksmuseum, Amsterdam, Netherlands, http://hdl.handle.net/10934/RM0001.COLLECT.295531

Wilhelm Trübner, 1878, Caesar at the Rubicon, Oil on canvas, 48.5 × 61.5 cm, Belvedere Museum, Vienna, Austria, https://sammlung.belvedere.at/objects/10015/caesar-am-rubicon